She's Done Pretending

A Memoir

NIKI BERGLER

LITTLE CREEK PRESS®
AND BOOK DESIGN
MINERAL POINT, WISCONSIN

Little Creek Press
5341 Sunny Ridge Road
Mineral Point, WI 53565

To contact author: connectwithme@nikibergler.com

ORDERING INFORMATION
Quantity sales. Special discounts are available on quantity purchases by corporations, associations, and others. For details, contact info@littlecreekpress.com

Orders by US trade bookstores and wholesalers.
Please contact Little Creek Press or Ingram for details.

Printed in the United States of America

Cataloging-in-Publication Data
Names: Bergler, Niki, author
Title: She's Done Pretending
Description: Mineral Point, WI. Little Creek Press, 2023
Identifiers: LCCN: 2022919936 | ISBN:
Subjects: BIOGRAPHY & AUTOBIOGRAPHY / Personal Memoirs

Book design by Mimi Bark and Little Creek Press

This is a work of creative non-fiction. All of the events in this memoir are true to the best of the author's memory. Some names and identifying features have been changed to protect the identity of certain parties. The author in no way represents any company, corporation, or brand, mentioned herein. The views expressed in this memoir are solely those of the author.

There is a saying: his version, her version, and the truth. As a life coach, I understand this fully. Our perspective is shaped by what we see, hear, and have experienced. This accumulation of knowledge creates what we interpret with each conversation and situation we encounter.

I do not have an eidetic memory, but I have often shocked my husband and friends with my ability to recover small details we have shared—usually involving food. I love food.

The memories I am sharing with you are how I remember them. Are they one hundred percent accurate? I believe so, but I acknowledge the mind processes and recalls the best it can.

I have no intention or desire here to hurt anyone. I only want to use my experiences to help others feel connected and empowered to face whatever story keeps them up at night. We all have one.

CONTENT WARNING: This book contains graphic descriptions of violence and sexual, emotional and physical abuse of a child, which may be difficult and triggering for some. I am not trying to convince you to avoid reading this book. I am being transparent to help protect your heart and mind.

While I was attending a Social Deviance class in college, our professor gave us the assignment to write a story and present our creativity to our class at the end of the semester. My initial excitement for the project dissipated as time passed with no regard for my writer's block. Panic snuffed out my confidence until a fellow student suggested, "Write what you know."

So, I did. I wrote a story called *Forgotten*. I shared my story in a way that would not expose me, as I was not ready to face whatever darkness would surface from my truth.

I am ready now. This is my story.

Chapter 1

"If there's a book that you want to read, but it hasn't
been written yet, then you must write it."

—TONI MORRISON

Before I was old enough to read or write, I had a passion
for adventurous tales and never-ending questions.
No matter the cost, I wanted to find the hidden cave,
discover the treasure, create a bond with friends that would
last a lifetime, and even eventually kiss the frog. The cost
usually resulted in me getting into trouble unless I was
with Grandma.

When I would visit my grandmother, the escapades were
endless, but as I grew, things like school and homework got
in the way of my adventures. Instead, my grandma, a grade-
school teacher, had me sit at the kitchen table and work on
writing, reading, math, etc.

One day, she pulled me from my homework to show me
how to mail a letter.

"You'll need to know this when you are older," she said.

The sun shone on the white envelope as her black pen
brought the address to life.

"Never use a red pen. Lick the back of the stamp, and you have to stick it right in the corner, here."

Though email is more manageable, I still stick the stamp in the upper right corner now and then, excited that the recipient would find my letter amongst their junk mail.

Grandma sealed the envelope while I wandered back to the table, bored, wanting to go outside and find my magical door to Narnia. The math problems on my paper meshed into one giant wall that kept me from freedom. I started daydreaming about scenes of the ultimate adventures. I could sit for hours looking busy and never finish one math problem.

Grandma noticed my love for adventures and thought I would like to write them down. She handed me my first journal when I was about eight years old. I filled the pages with ridiculous ramblings of a young girl who would travel the world and someday marry Jim Carrey. Writing became my escape. Believe it or not, I needed an escape by eight years old.

My father obliterated my future wild and limitless dreams when he found my secret journal hiding under my mattress, unbeknownst to me, a familiar hiding spot for most children. He read aloud my words to all and ridiculed the profound young emotions I had written between those light blue lines. I stood mortified near a wall, using it to prop me up while my family laughed at me.

Though I was embarrassed, my love for writing would not die so quickly. Still, I couldn't risk my father finding my voice on paper again. I would write short stories, poems, and songs to my perfection, then shred them. I couldn't bear the thought of someone telling me again what a pathetic loser I was. Looking back, I understand why my father could have interpreted my writing as a threat. There were certain things he wouldn't want people to know about us.

WHEN I WAS IN FOURTH GRADE, our class took a trip to the library directly across from the school. As I walked through the doors of this library, I felt the hair on my arms raise in excitement. There was a strange smell that brought me a calmness, and it craved nurturing. You know what I mean if you have ever sniffed a book and liked it.

The walls were covered from floorboard to ceiling in stories, endless adventures. It was overwhelming. Where was I to start? With the suggestion of a classmate, I began with Garfield, written by Jim Davis. I would grab a dozen books, more than I could read at a time, and lay on the worn carpet by the old fireplace, which had not felt the heat of a flame in years.

I found myself at the library almost every day—another escape. My father stated I was too stupid to read and did not believe I was spending my time there. He thought I was lying and going somewhere else, so he grounded me. I had to come straight home after school.

The next day, I started venting to one of my teachers, yelling, "It's not fair! They always tell me I am bad and finally do something good, but now I am not allowed to do that!"

I had felt proud of who I was when I was in the library.

My teacher informed me I could bring as many books home as I liked; I just needed to sign them out. I perked up. I planned to run to the library after school to grab as many books as I could carry and then hustle home so I wouldn't get in trouble.

I gathered my books and brought them to the front desk to check out. The librarian asked for my library card.

"I don't have a library card."

"Okay, have your parents sign this, and when you bring it back, we will get you a card."

Once again, I felt defeated. My heart sunk into my chest. Not only was I not able to get my books, but if I took any more time putting them away, I would be late getting home.

There was no way my father was going to sign for a card. So, while my dad was busy, I had my stepmother sign the slip the librarian had handed me before I flew out the door to run home.

The next day, I was issued a card, borrowed as many books as possible, and walked the five blocks home, huffing and puffing over the bag's weight. I didn't care about the weight or the difficulty in carrying my books home; they were my trophies. Even when my father became upset that I had still found a way, I smiled with satisfaction. I was so proud of my bag of books.

After a couple of years of borrowing every Garfield book, Goosebumps book, or Archie comic one hundred times over, I asked the young front desk lady with long brown, curly hair if she would recommend something different. I remember the sly smile curving over her lips, her eyes squinting as she sized me up. She repeated my words back to me, "Something different? How old are you?"

I lied. I felt small, so I told her I was thirteen because that was so much older than my eleven-year-old self.

I'm sure she knew I was lying. Regardless, her feet started walking in a new direction, so I followed her. She began to rattle off the names of writers she enjoyed. I don't remember what she said because I focused on the thick books we passed. I had never been on this side of the library. It made me feel small, insecure, and intimidated. I started thinking perhaps I shouldn't have lied about my age. Maybe I wasn't ready for whatever she was about to give me.

Suddenly, the librarian stopped and reached her hand out to snatch a book off the shelf. With a broad smile, she handed me the first novel that would make me fall madly in love with reading—*Loves Music, Loves to Dance*, by Mary Higgins Clark. "Here. You'll like this," she said.

I held the book in my hand and looked back up at the girl in disbelief. "Are you kidding me?" I replied. "This is going to take me years to read; it's huge! I can't read this!"

She shrugged her shoulders and replied, "Then don't," and walked away like a boss, leaving the book in my hand and my jaw on the floor.

After a few minutes of suffering from shock, I accepted her unspoken saucy challenge. I borrowed the book and finished it much faster than I had believed I could. My confidence in my abilities grew.

I searched for more adventures and began to check out more than books from the library. I checked out of my home, body, and the newly developed voice inside my head that hated me like everyone else.

Over the years, I traveled, died, lived, caught the bad guy, and fell in love. After each book, I would retell the story my way, but I never wrote it down. I blocked the strong desire to create a new world on paper. That is until the rotating sun and moon launched me into my twenties, and I found Lisa Jackson.

Lisa Jackson became one of my favorite authors. I found the beginning of her suspenseful Die series on a spinning bookshelf at a dusty gas station in Silver Bay, Minnesota, a small town of about 1,700 people. I took the book back to our campsite and started reading. I fell into the book quickly. My brows were stuck together in concentration for hours as I tried to discover the killer before the big reveal. The killer evaded me the whole time—unheard of! No one had stumped me as a reader before.

Although I read the book while on vacation, I needed a vacation redo. I did not feel rested and ready to return to work; I felt more like I needed therapy. So many emotions from the book bounced off the walls of my mind. Lisa's work was perfection. It poured gas on the tiny ember I could never wholly snuff out.

Words pieced together in my mind, and once again, I was overwhelmed with the urge to write. I found myself narrating stories while watching people go about their business. My fingers feverishly typed as my creativity flowed. My adrenaline pumped as I painted a picture with the words I chose to sew together, but then I'd hit *delete*.

After five or so years of writing and deleting, a sound began to haunt my consciousness. A voice that started as a whisper but got louder as time went on. It said I could not create my imaginary world on paper until I accepted the journey of writing my story first.

How does someone begin to write a book about their childhood abuse? I'm guessing it's probably different for each person. Exposing my deepest secrets and insecurities was not on the table until I was willing to accept my past could heal present hearts. My experience required courage when I feared rejection and abandonment, grace toward myself when I couldn't type one more word, hope my story would help someone feel connected and heard, many tears, and lots of chocolate.

I am thankful my story drew you in. This adventure may provoke strong emotions as I give myself to you. I am genuinely sorry about this. We live in a broken world. If you feel broken, I hope sharing this chapter of my life can help mend a piece of your heart and give you the strength to fight for your future. There is a reason you are reading this book. My wish is my nightmare gives you courage, comfort, and permission to own your story.

I want to emphasize *nightmare* to warn you it may be triggering. My story shares detailed accounts of my physical, sexual, and emotional abuse. If you find it too much, there is no shame in asking for help. I did. I had to. Writing this book has been an incredible growth journey. I could not have done it alone.

I often needed to remind myself that I am not who I am because of my abuse but who I am despite it. What I thought was a curse has become my blessing because I can now meet people where they are and help them walk forward. That is how my coaching business, Forward Focus LLC, was birthed into this world in 2019.

I am sure I do not have to tell you that pain does not dissipate when we leave the physical place where everything went down. Memories are like a sticky spiderweb; you grasp at it with one hand to get it off, but it just sticks to whatever it touches.

The memories I expose are not for revenge. There is no anger here, only healing. I acknowledge the abuse I endured, which wounded more than my soul alone. I am not sharing my story to cause pain to others who were a part of my life during my childhood or when I struggled to hold my head up as a young adult.

Some ask, why share? Why bring up the past? Why focus on the bad? Can't you just let it go?

That's just it. I am no longer focused on the past or myself.

I have written my story to connect with those intimate with the sting abuse can cause. You are in good company if you are drowning in rage, pain, betrayal, shame, guilt, and disgust. I want you to know there is peace, love, hope, inspiration, connection, certainty, and a future. If you are in a storm, it's time to find your calm amongst the waves. It is time to find yourself, possibly for the first time.

If there were only one thing I would want you to know, it would be that what happened to you is not your fault. You have been holding onto shame and guilt that is not yours to carry. Nothing was wrong with you, nothing different, nothing you could have done to stop it. What happened to you has everything to do with who hurt you, not who you are.

Forgive yourself for all of the anger, pain, and shame you have been holding. You are strong. The abusers of the world should be afraid because we are all free to choose in life, but we are not free from the consequences of our choices.

If you have stumbled upon my book out of curiosity and have no history of abuse, you are welcome here too. I am glad you are here. Thank you for taking the time to read my story. I can assure you, whether you know it or not, someone in your life is hurting far more than they are letting on. This book may allow you to understand them and help them open up and free themselves.

We all have more power than we realize, and it's time we tap into it.

Chapter 2

"Our wounds are often the openings into the best and most beautiful parts of us."

—DAVID RICHO

I am a pro at fooling people into believing I am happy. If you smile, say the right things, and show a lot of energy, people will never ask if you are okay. One thing I have learned is most of us are not okay.

On some level, I believed I deserved the pain as penance for who I was. My pain gave me the illusion I was protecting myself. If I didn't hold on to pain, mistrust, or anger, how would I keep people from hurting me in the future? But the thing was, people were still hurting me, and worse yet, I was hurting myself. I needed help.

My doctor referred me to Sarah after I had raised some concerns about stress and depression. She suggested medication for the anxiety, but I declined. I had taken medication before and was still miserable and depressed. This time, like a natural birth, my goal was to be born again without a prescription. As much as I begged for the pain to stop when no one was looking, I would make sure I felt every bit of it now so I could get over it once and for all.

My stubbornness did not propel me into action. I carried the digits my doctor gave me for three months. Each time I dialed the number written on the torn piece of white paper, my anxiety increased, and I slammed my finger on the off button. I'd wait a minute, silently hoping they wouldn't call me back as if I had dialed 911. No one ever returned my hang-up calls.

After I fought the crippling vulnerability of telling someone I needed help, the receptionist informed me I would need to wait another three months before I could get in to see Sarah. Part of me was upset. I had finally developed the courage to move forward, and I was afraid if I waited too long, my courage would deflate like an abandoned balloon.

I pushed my thoughts and the appointment out of my mind. However, in a flash, the meeting was on my schedule for the next day. Time is a fickle illusion. I know because it never moves fast when I am doing burpees.

I told a few friends about my plans. I would have rather suffered in silence, but I figured if my friends knew what I was doing, they would ask me how it went, and I'd have felt like a drama queen if I told them I bailed.

I was thirty-two years old when I met Sarah, a therapist, for the first time. I was a mercurial character when it came to seeking therapy. There had been other therapists before this one, but I'd developed a pattern of walking out halfway through my first appointments. They were all idiots, or so I said. Maybe they were. Perhaps I didn't give them a chance.

I arrived at my appointment on time, got through the solid clinic doors, passed the overwhelming scent of cleaner, and checked in. I was proud of myself.

The chair I chose faced all the doors so I could see anyone

entering, but it was angled so I could avoid eye contact if necessary. I sat in the waiting room, staring at the scenery pictures hung on the cream-colored wall. Difficulties I had faced these last few years clicked through my mind as I changed the channel from one memory to the next.

Flashbacks and nightmares were becoming the norm. I was experiencing back-to-back anxiety attacks, which I believed were heart attacks, but the doctors assured me I was still alive.

That word, "alive." Was I living?

Each day my stomach found a new reason to swirl and evacuate all contents in my colon at a rapid, painful rate. I sought out the bathroom wherever I went to ensure a fast exit if needed. I was often dizzy, tired, and panicky. I was afraid to leave my house. There were no more football parties and outdoor adventures, and I was in no condition to try something new or travel. I could barely get through work, and school was exhausting. I hardly call that living.

A soft but manly voice interrupted my thoughts.

"Isn't it beautiful outside?"

My attention landed on a grown man wearing a dress and a wig, his makeup whimsical. His, though I believe he would prefer I say her, so I will, her attention was on me. I stared back dumbfounded, not because she looked different but because she was talking to me in a therapist's office. I could be crazy, you know.

My inner dialogue chimed in. *You've got to be kidding me. Are you really going to strike up a conversation with me right now? We are in a therapist's office. Isn't there some law against this? What makes you think I am in any mood to talk about the damn weather? Or to speak at all, for that matter!*

Instead of sharing my thoughts, I smiled and said, "Yes,

it is a beautiful day. Do you have plans to enjoy it later?"

"Oh yes!" The volume of her voice increased as her excitement rose, and she started rattling off more information than I cared to hear. "I am going ... I'm not from around here. Once I ..."

Her voice danced in and out of my consciousness. I didn't want to be rude or dismissive. She seemed like a nice person, and under different circumstances, I bet I would have enjoyed hearing her story, but I was too busy fighting all the excuses to pick up and run.

"Jamie?"

"Op, that's me!" she said as she bounced up and pranced out of view.

Will I ever be that happy? I asked myself. *Doubt it.*

"Niki?"

An older woman with soft blond hair and blue eyes stood before me. Something about her seemed familiar, though I had never met her before. A sudden peace came over me. In that instance, I felt confident I had made the right choice. *Maybe I would be as happy as Jamie.*

THUS FAR, all Sarah and I had accomplished was creating a foundation for our new relationship. The one where I spill all my secrets, and she promises not to tell. She told me I could trust her, and I readily accepted her assurance because no one before her had ever betrayed my trust. Sarcasm is another gift I possess.

Since my progress would not happen overnight, Sarah taught me quick tools to help me deal with the anxiety attacks. She also informed me that I would feel more anxious as we moved the past information around my head.

"More anxiety?" I spoke. "Awesome. So much for therapy helping."

She chuckled at my dry humor.

She explained how the brain worked and processed information. I appreciated this. I am a sucker for learning how things work. She showed me EFT (emotional freedom technique), guided imagery, breathing techniques, and so forth.

Our foundation solidified over time. Sarah became aware of the basic history of my past. She now knew where my family line started and, for the most part, ended. Sarah needed to take notes to keep up with the family tree. She was not the first one to have to make a chart.

Now and then, I would share with Sarah what I considered a mild experience from my past. I was careful when I spoke, watching her face for a micro-movement that would reveal how much I could genuinely share with her. Sarah was attentive, but I stayed tuned to any indication it was time to walk out of the room and tell her she was an idiot.

She never flinched as I shared my story.

"You have PTSD," she said

Suddenly I was flooded with fear. I felt trapped. Every cop show flashed through my mind. *What was I thinking coming here! PTSD is the kind of thing that gets put on your permanent record. If anything terrible happens in the future, they'll blame it on me and the PTSD. Oh, she was mentally sick. We should have seen this coming. We can't trust her—she has PTSD and might lose it!*

It was as if she had labeled me incapable of control and with a wounded mind. I realized for the first time the stereotypes of PTSD floating around in my head. I had never given it much thought before. Much like the stereotype, only the weak seek therapy. *Maybe I am overreacting. There is nothing I can do about it now. Onto my permanent record it will go. You may as well keep going with this.*

"PTSD, that's a thing war vets have, right? Understandably so, I can't imagine the things they have seen and the things they have had to do," I responded.

"I can't imagine all of the things you have seen and the things you have had to do," she said.

Her words hit me like a ton of bricks.

Whoa, you can't compare like that. Vets are heroes. They are the strongest, fastest, most calculating, most courageous warriors. If I were strong like them, then maybe I wouldn't be so afraid all the time.

"I am no hero."

Sarah watched me for a bit, then pulled out a sheet labeled, "What would I feel if I were not feeling shame and guilt?" She asked me to write and work through seven moments in my life I would say were defining and bring my answers to our next visit.

She gave me an assignment. I was not impressed.

I ignored the sheet, but the question burned in the back of my mind each day when I was doing the dishes, shopping for clothes, and even while working.

What would I be feeling if I were not feeling shame?

Why do I keep asking myself this? Shame. Why would I be feeling shame? I'm not the one who abused a child. That sick fuck should be the one feeling shame. I bet he doesn't. Wait, do I feel shame? Anger maybe. What? No, this is stupid. I don't feel guilty. She's got this all wrong. What did I say that made her think I felt shame? Why would she give me that sheet? It's clear she is not going to be able to help me. I screwed up. I'm just going to cancel my next appointment. I knew this was a mistake.

My unwanted thoughts were distracting. They spun around my mind like a carousel, the same endless tune with different animals representing the questions I could not answer. I was not able to focus on work. I was edgy and defensive. Sarah made my problems worse!My next appointment finally arrived, and I was intense. My foot tapped the waiting room floor as if sending a warning through Morse code. That stupid sheet of paper had unveiled a startling discovery: I could not define my emotions. I did not know how to articulate what I felt. I couldn't even nail down how I was feeling at that moment!

Sarah came into the waiting room to get me. Our eyes locked, and my feet landed hard on the carpet as I stood up. With shoulders back, I swiftly moved past her as I led the way to her office.

As soon as she closed the door, I ranted, "This is bullshit! I don't feel shame. None of it was my fault! And guilt! That son of a bitch should be the one feeling guilt! I was just a kid!" I yelled out, partially aware that everyone on the floor may have just labeled me crazy again.

"You're right," she said. "You have been holding onto shame and guilt that is not yours to hold."

My anger turned to anguish. I couldn't pinpoint my body's pain as everything seemed heavy. I tried to inhale as I fell into the chair beneath me, but even the air felt thick.

It wasn't mine to hold.

With no witty comeback, no angry retort, I acknowledged my distress and attempted to accept the wheel of emotions that makes us human. *I do feel shame. I am disgusted, rageful, scared, sad, lonely, wallowing in contempt, and bitter.*

"Where would you like to start today?" she asked,

breaking through my thoughts as she walked to her chair and sat down.

I felt sick to my stomach, and my chest felt like it was weighing it down further. Moisture pooled at the corner of my eyes until gravity guided it down my cheeks. I took a deep breath.

I can do this. I can do this. I can do this.

As if a marionettist were holding my strings, my body propped up in the oversized chair. Our eyes met, and I sighed through my response. "I guess we should start at the beginning."

Chapter 3

"When I was very young, most of my childhood heroes
wore capes, flew through the air, or picked up buildings
with one arm. They were spectacular and got a lot of
attention. But as I grew, my heroes changed, so that
now I can honestly say that anyone who does
anything to help a child is a hero to me."

—FRED ROGERS

I t was not hard for me to track down my medical records.
When I read the hospital-provided tale of baby Niki, the
information had me laughing in self-love and crying
from a place of unknown pain. The nurses' detailed notes
helped me connect to a part of me I didn't know was lost.

I wish I could remember these perfect
strangers instead of the darker
memories that flash like lightning.

I was a beautiful, healthy baby
girl, weighing eight pounds one
ounce. Even as a baby, I had a
dramatic entrance as my petite

frame slid onto a pile of poo in a Texas hospital. With a full head of brown hair, brown eyes, a button nose, soft light olive skin, and what I've gathered to be the cutest little fingers and toes. God molded me, using pieces from my mother's generation and parts of my father's to create an adorable little me.

My mother had soft pale skin, dark brown eyes, and wavy brown hair. She was a young twenty-two-year-old seductress. She had been married previously and had two beautiful girls.

My father was twenty-three years old. He was tall, with muscular arms, dark brown hair, brown eyes, and light olive skin. My mother once told me he was fun, adventurous, and loved fried chicken—the meal she made him on their first date.

When I asked my mother how our story began, she painted the picture of a struggling family. She said we were homeless, living under a viaduct in Texas. We had no food, no place to live, and no idea how we would get out. She wanted my father to ask for help from his father, so we could find a place to live. But, she said my father and grandfather were not getting along.

As a young girl, I soaked up every word she spoke. As I got older, I noticed she had a knack for embellishing, so I will never know how much truth was in the tales she spun.

My father says we never lived on the streets. He said we weren't in Texas long. He left his father's house when he turned eighteen, admitting they did not see eye to eye then. First, he took off to California, the trip where he met my mother. They then ended up in Texas together. It wasn't long before I was born, and they moved back to Wisconsin to be around family.

I am willing to bet one of my father and grandfather's fights had something to do with my mother's pregnancy before marriage. I discovered this little nugget on Google in my early twenties. Google informed me my parents were married just a few months before I was born and not long after her previous divorce was finalized.

The long-told fairy tale about my young and in love parents wanting and trying for a third child was a lie. For some reason, finding out I was not planned hurt me in a way I didn't expect. Maybe I would have felt different if they had told me the truth from the beginning.

In an attempt to understand where I come from and why my parents made the decision they did, I have so many questions. Did my mother get pregnant to trap him? Were they planning on having a baby, but I came sooner than expected? Did he fall madly in love with her, promise her family but change his mind? Was she just a one-night stand? Was he? When did she tell him she had two kids and a soon-to-be ex-husband? How well did they really know each other before I changed the course of their lives?

My parents decided to move back to Wisconsin when I was just over eleven months old—perhaps searching for a new start.

Shortly after we arrived in Wisconsin, one of my hospital records showed a one-year checkup that indicated I was an ordinary, healthy girl. At twelve months old, I was walking, described as *"increasingly independent." "Mom describes consistently good appetite."* I assure you that has not changed. *"She sleeps through the night, developing mentally, walks and runs with good balance, climbs onto the chair, turns book pages, and mimics household chores. Language, approximately five to ten words, beginning to combine two words."* Okay, now I am just bragging.

My memories come as flashes at this time in my life. I was almost two, it was winter, and we lived in a large brick home on the edge of a hill near Grandma and Grandpa's house. The house sat tall, overlooking the small town, which at the time held one bar and one small grocery store.

This home was an old schoolhouse until the sixties, when someone renovated and rented it as apartments. A few years later, it was bought and turned into an Amish museum. After some time, a new owner purchased and restored the building into apartments again.

Winter in Wisconsin means snow, so my tiny body was snug tight in a snowsuit and boots. My tush imprinted in the snow beneath me. Two huskies named Bandit and Red were keeping me company. I am unsure if they belonged to one of the neighbors or us. This is my only memory of these two sweet pups. I can still feel their soft furry fluff between my tiny fingers and see their piercing eyes. Even at such a young age, I recall having so much love for them.

ANOTHER FLASH, I must have been around three years old. There was an event happening at my older sister's school. I don't recall why they were putting it on, perhaps a firefighters' fundraiser. Each classroom had an activity and a chance to win prizes. The eighth-grade awards were the best. Cake. Frozen cake. Cupcakes. Small cakes, large cakes, white cakes, blue cakes. Oh, how I love me some cake.

My father thought it was a waste of money to enter us in the game and yelled at my mother for spending it frivolously. He asked why she wouldn't just buy a cake. "It would be cheaper!" he snarled in the hallway.

"It's about the memories, the experience, the moment," my mother fought back. My sisters and I stood near the lockers, ashamed of the tension that thickened the air between them. Both seemed oblivious to the hall filled with students, teachers, and parents.

After their argument, my mother, sisters, and I went to the eighth-grade room. On the floor was a circle made from colorful tape, with prizes inside. The best description I can give is spin the bottle with the award being cake instead of kisses. So yeah, way better.

My oldest sister did win! My mother, sisters, and I were so excited. We danced and celebrated as if it were our wishing that granted us a cake. My mother thought our father would be excited too, but he was not. Instead, he held fast to his anger and belief that our experience was a waste of money.

We lived in a trailer court next to the school, so we girls walked home together. I don't recall why my father didn't join us. We hadn't seen much of him all night. He was a volunteer firefighter. Perhaps he volunteered that night at the school.

My mother held the cake, which upset my oldest sister, who felt she should carry her winnings. My other sister walked silently. Then there was me, dancing down the street because we were going to have cake no matter how late it was as far as I was concerned.

My mother gave us a pep talk on how we were all on the same team, so we were all winners. She proudly told us as long as we were together, we could do anything. "Nothing will tear us apart," she promised.

Did she know what was coming? Was she ignoring the signs, or was she just as ignorant as the beautiful young girls who hung on her every word?

Chapter 4

"Sometimes God will deliver you from the fire,
and other times God will make you fireproof."

—JOEL OSTEEN

Just before I was three years old, we moved out of the
large building with the huskies and into a trailer in a
new town nearby. It had two bedrooms, with the rooms
on opposite sides of the trailer, and a small kitchen area,
bathroom, and living room occupied the space in between.
I don't remember a TV or entertainment center. We did
not have toys in our room. I am sure my parents were still
trying to create a life and home.

When we had first moved in, my sisters and I occupied
the room at the farthest end of the trailer. This room was
right next to the bathroom. One night I woke up to sounds
I had never heard before. I whispered to my sisters to see
if they were up. They both were and told me in a hushed
tone to be quiet. "They are playing a game," my sister said.

In a flash, I lit up with excitement. "I love games!" I said.

My sister suddenly realized her mistake and quickly
hushed me again.

A feeling came over me as I lay in our bunk bed, listening to the strange sounds. I was scared. Something didn't feel right. After much under-our-breath arguing, I decided against my sister's plea for me to sleep and crawled out of bed to go to the bathroom. I tiptoed into the hall. The bathroom was the first door on the left, right before the living room where my mother and father were.

I knew I had made a mistake when my father's voice cut through the darkness. My body raced on the inside but froze on the outside. He was furious I was out of bed. I stammered the words explaining I needed to go to the bathroom, but I didn't feel his anger subsiding as his footsteps grew closer.

Through the darkness pitched my mom's pleading voice.

"No, it's okay. I'll take care of it," she said.

I still could not see anything but imagined she was holding him back because the footsteps had stopped. He continued to speak of how bad a child I was when my mother suddenly appeared naked on her knees before me.

"It's okay," she whispered. Our faces were so close I could feel her breath.

"But I'm scared," I whispered back.

"Go to the bathroom and head back to bed." Her voice got louder as she said, "And girls, you make sure she stays there." My sisters' voices erupted from our room as they defended themselves against the unspoken accusation. My father's voice boomed in the home, again silencing my sisters. I quickly went to the bathroom and ran back to our room.

Shortly after that night, my father moved everything in our room to the other end of the trailer.

MY MOTHER WORKED at a gas station down the street. My father worked a night-shift job at a bakery. I was too young for school yet, but my sisters attended one a stone's throw from our trailer. Since we could see the single-story, light tan brick building from our home, my mother and I would watch them walk to school.

My father came home in the morning before my mother left for work. I was to stay in my room alone and be very quiet. My father would go to sleep immediately upon arriving home, and I was not allowed to wake him up.

There was nothing for me to do throughout the day. My spirit craved adventure. I needed to explore and run my imagination. I also required a lot of attention. It is pretty easy for a child like me to make dangerous mistakes. This was one that still haunts me.

My mother smoked. One of our favorite ways to pass the hot summer day was to make ashtrays using mud. We picked up old cigarette butts on the ground and pushed them into the tray's rim to make divots. Doing this would give the cigarette a place to sit when the smoker was not holding it. The final step was leaving them in the sun to harden and hoping they wouldn't crumble. There was a wet-to-dry ratio that, when used correctly, would prevent our dirt trays from falling apart.

One night my sisters and I were playing in our room. My older sister grabbed my mother's cigarette lighter and started lighting the fuzz on our socks. She had learned this magic trick from another family member. She was seven years old at the time. We thought we were so cool practicing "magic" until our mother came in hotter than the lighter.

We figured she'd be impressed if she understood better, so we showed her how cool it was! My sister placed the lighter under her heel and pulled back the rough igniter until the flame appeared above the metal guide to create a wave of gentle heat as the fire crawled up the sock before it extinguished itself. Even my mother had to admit it was pretty neat to watch. But she returned her lighter to the drawer and told us never to do it again.

This new trick pumped us up, not knowing what we were doing was dangerous. My sisters understood the danger after Mom had talked to us, or at least, they stopped being so excited about it, but I was three years old and was not old enough to understand just how much magic fire possessed.

The following day, the girls went to school, my mother went to work, and my dad slept in his room after working a night shift. I was bored. I wanted to have fun again.

I went into the kitchen to see if my mother's lighter was still in the drawer. I crept across the room, careful not to make a sound. The old, stubborn drawer squeaked a little and caused me to suck in my breath for fear that I had awakened my father. When I was sure I could hear my dad sleeping, I peeked inside the drawer. The lighter was in the same spot.

My excitement grew as I snatched it up and ran back into our room. I plopped my tush on the floor, lifted my leg, ignited the lighter, and moved it so the flame could reach the bottom of my socks.

A problem I had not anticipated revealed itself. I was still wearing the socks from the previous night, and all the fuzz was gone.

I wasn't giving up so quickly. I put on a fresh pair of socks, but that pair didn't have any fluff either. My magic trick was not working. I looked around the room for something we had not lit the night before. Our blanket caught my eye.

I struck the lighter on the corner of the quilt and watched it light up, floating on top as if it wasn't even touching it. I squealed in glee as the fuzz burned and extinguished itself.

But then, the next corner caught faster than the other. I watched as the flame began to spread over the blanket, touching and moving quickly. This time it was leaving little bright orange spots as it spread. Panic surged through my body. Somehow, I knew this wasn't good. I tried to blow it out. I tried shaking the blanket. Before I knew it, the fire engulfed the quilt covering our bed.

I ran past the kitchen, living room, and bathroom to my father's room and tried to wake him up. I called to him, pushed on his shoulders, and wanted him to understand I had done something terrible. He was immediately irritated and yelled at me to lie down.

I tried again, telling him the house was on fire, but the more words I pushed through my twisted tongue, the angrier he became. I drove back harder until he yelled louder than the screams coming from my head.

"If you don't go lay down, I am going to whoop your ass," he said, then mumbled incoherently under his breath as he rolled over.

I ran to the corner of his room and curled into a ball on the floor.

Seconds later, the fire alarms beeped a deafening high-pitched warning that smoke was present. My hands shot up and pressed hard against my ears.

My father sprang from his bed and raced down the hall. He was too late. He ran back to his bedroom, grabbed me (thank you), and rushed us outside. The neighbors were already coming out of their homes. My father put me in someone else's arms and told them to watch me while he ran down to the fire station, a couple of blocks away, to get help.

At the time, I did not see him run down the street. I thought he had gone back into the house. The neighbor who was supposed to watch me was occupied by telling the other neighbors all he had seen so far. I remember feeling overwhelmed with fear that my father was still in the trailer, so I ran back in. I was screaming for him while my mind raced through panicked thoughts. Where was he? Can't he hear me? Why can't I see anything?

No one answered my cries. The crackling and shifting of the burning trailer around me made it so I could barely hear my voice, let alone anyone else's.

Our home filled quickly with gray-white smoke, a blazing fire roaring near my ears, consuming what little we had. My throat and eyes burned as I searched desperately, thinking I would never see him again.

The smoke smothered my face making it difficult to breathe or open my eyes. I dropped to my knees, taken down by all that was happening.

I was in the hallway with my knees and palms on the floor when I felt someone's arms wrap around my waist and lift me high. My hero spoke, and though I couldn't understand him, I knew it was my father. He flipped me to face him. I wrapped my arms around his neck and my legs around his chest. I laid my head on his shoulder and breathlessly asked if hell was coming up from under us. My imagination took over as I pictured flashes of the earth shifting and rising under the trailer as he brought me out of the house again.

Police officers, fire trucks, and an ambulance surrounded our block. I was put in the back of the ambulance and given an oxygen mask that I kept dropping. My arms were like lead, and every time the EMT would lift my arm to hold the cover over my mouth, my arm would give out and fall to my lap. I am unaware if my weakness was due to damage to my body or the stress of the situation.

I could hear the other EMTs talking. They said I would be fine after a bit. I was young and didn't sustain any damage from which my body wouldn't heal.

I took it all in. My father yelled at the neighbor that I had almost died because he didn't watch me. Our home crumbled to the ground, and black smoke filled the sky and eventually, my mother's scream, her tears, and the horror of the soon-to-be dust pile that was once our home.

Some neighbors comforted and consoled my parents, telling them they would help in any way possible. Others watched the whole scene in morbid curiosity.

As an adult, I still cannot imagine the emotional range of that experience. Watching your home burn to the ground, almost losing your daughter twice, having no sleep, and knowing your daughter caused the loss. It is a lot to handle. I am so sorry I caused that painful day.

Our life started to piece back together. Little memories here and there flicker. We stayed with one of our neighbors for a short time but got bed bugs. They burrow under your skin and itch uncontrollably. Eventually, my parents purchased a new trailer down the street. This one seemed bigger. The bedrooms were on the same end of the trailer, and the kitchen had a large front window bringing in natural light. Neighbors continued to help wherever possible, donating mattresses, clothes, and food.

Things were getting better, but there was still much tension in the home. My father's voice was getting louder, sharper, and more impatient. I remember my mother rocking me to sleep one evening and my father impatiently yelling at her, telling her I was too old.

"Put her down! You're spoiling her!" he'd say. I was almost four.

"She is fine!" my mother would snap back.

I felt safe with her. Life began to shift, though, like the wind before a storm. I was getting older, and I was starting to understand something dark was developing in our home.

Chapter 5

"Nobody wants to get locked up, although 'locked up' is a matter of perspective. There can be people who are in prison mentally and emotionally and worse off than those who are behind bars."

—WESLEY SNIPES

All three of us girls shared a large bed in our new trailer. I was around four years old, my older sister would have been around six, and the eldest would have been about eight years old.

One of my sisters had started to wet the bed while we slept. This new development had set off a rage in my father we had never seen before. After repeated "offenses," my father forced my sister to sleep in the closet on a pile of dirty clothes. If she wet herself at night, she had to wear those clothes for the day after a good whoopin'. I do not know if my mother was aware he was forcing this punishment.

After a few nights of no accidents, we awoke to my sister lying in the closet. She was curled into a ball, tightly squeezing a load of dirty laundry, and would not make eye contact with us. Shame, guilt, and fear clung to her face. The energy she put out had me on edge, and I didn't particularly appreciate how it felt. I couldn't leave well enough alone. I pressed and pressed her to speak to us until she broke and confirmed our suspicion. She had wet herself in the night.

She was scared and begged me not to tell my father. She pleaded with only me as I was the weakest link in the pack. I told her not to worry. Dad would realize it was an accident, and everything would be okay. He would understand. I went to find him so he could make her feel better. I was very, very wrong.

My father came in screaming, grabbed her tiny arm, lifted her into the air, and started beating her with his other hand. She screamed wildly as hateful words flew from his mouth while he shook and beat her. Her eyes remained shut as her head flopped left and right, and terrifying sounds escaped her mouth.

Time seemed to stand still and speed up at that exact moment. My other sister and I watched in horror as the punishment unfolded. Neither of us could move as the fear was too intense.

My heart filled with guilt and shame. How could I have made such a mistake?

He crossed a line. Sure, he had given us whoopins throughout our short lives, but this was different. He went too far.

I let out a scream as my sister wailed. Her head fell back as she choked and gasped for air. Her body became limp like a rag doll. I grabbed his big arm, pulling and screaming, begging him to stop. My mother came in at that time, wrapped her petite frame around his back, and somehow pulled him out into the hallway.

He let go of my sister and turned his anger toward our mother, pushing her against the wall. He screamed at her for her "stupid daughter who couldn't get herself up in the middle of the night to use the restroom." He yelled at my mother for not disciplining us enough.

"They're disrespectful and ungrateful. They need to learn," he said as he stormed down the hall.

My mother stood in the doorway, watching him with wide eyes. We watched her and waited for her to defend us. I thought she would comfort my sister the way she always had after his yelling, but instead, she turned toward us and showed a side of her I had never seen before. She tore into each of us, the mistakes we made, how spoiled we were. She sounded just like him. I think she was becoming afraid of him too.

After our mother left the room, I put my arms around my sister. I wanted to comfort her. Stunned, confused, and exhausted, she managed enough energy to push me away and give me a look of pure anger. She felt I had betrayed her. She and I were close. I followed her wherever she went, but she told me not to tell him, and I didn't listen.

Our other sister chimed in with the verbal lashing of how I ruined everything.

That day our lives, our trust as a family, and the feeling of safety started to crack.

The warm, safe bubble of a family I once clung to was starting to dissolve like cotton candy in water. Our foundation began to crumble. Tempers became shorter, and spankings became a daily thing. Nothing was good enough, done right, or fast enough. Tension grew in the home as we never knew which father we were getting each day or what we would do to set him off. On top of that, we no longer had our mother to console us. Sometimes, she made the problems worse.

MY MOTHER ENJOYED PRANKS. Dad did not appreciate them when he was the target.

One night, my mother wanted to scare my father. He was deathly afraid of spiders, and she had purchased a giant black tarantula spider bigger than my hand. The spider was fake but made to look real with its rubbery legs and soft center. It had a black plastic tube with a pump at the end. When someone squeezed the pump, it would push air through the line, and the spider would hop as if it were alive.

My father was in bed sleeping, my sisters were not home, and my mother thought it would be a perfect time to prank him. She set everything up. She sat me in the corner to watch. She carefully placed the spider on his shin and crouched at the edge of the bed. With a couple of squeezes, the spider came to life. It hopped up to his thigh and toward his face.

When he woke up to the spider moving on top of him, he let out a loud shriek and ran out of the room. When he heard my mother laughing, he put two and two together and returned to the room with fire in his eyes. Her prank did not have a happy ending.

Petrified, I snuck out of their room and pretended I had no idea what was happening.

SOMETIMES MY SISTERS were not around. I never understood where they went. The typical response to my question was that they were with "other family," but they weren't "my family," so I couldn't go.

When my sisters were home, chore duty increased. My father did not provide instructions on how to complete our tasks. We were told the job and expected to know what to do.

My father told us to clean the dishes one day while he and my mother napped. When we asked for instructions, he told us to figure it out. After much internal discussion, we decided each sister would perform a task: one would wash, one would dry, and the other would put away.

I was the smallest, so my sisters carried (ever so gently and quietly) a chair up to the sink and had me wash, which resulted in her handing me back the dishes to clean again and our other sister, bored, having no containers to put away.

Working in the kitchen together, we three girls figured out what flow worked best for us. We would bicker about who had the easier job. Our developing teamwork might have created a precious memory if we hadn't had to hear my father's voice yelling "quiet" even though we were already whispering.

The fun of the experience deteriorated when I learned a valuable lesson I have carried to this day. As it turns out, you are not supposed to wash a toaster in the sink. Thankfully the toaster was unplugged. While it may not have worked ever again, it was clean.

My father was not impressed with its cleanliness, however. Instead, we were all punished. Me because I had washed the toaster and the other girls for being "too stupid to stop me."

MY SISTERS AND I were home together during the summer. My father often left to go to the neighbor's house while my mother worked. He would put us in our room and lock the bedroom door to contain us while he was away.

Sometimes, hours would go by before we heard him come back, and his coming home didn't mean we would be free of our room. I recall peeing in the dirty laundry more than once and claiming ignorance when he questioned us about it.

My father instructed my older sister to clean under the bathroom sink. During that time, she discovered a hole in the wall that led to our room. The back of our dresser blocked the cave's entrance, but there was clearly a secret passage.

This discovery presented an adventure to us the next time we were locked in our room. We tried to move the dresser, but it was too heavy. So, we pulled the clothes out and then the drawers out. We tilted the frame down and had just enough room to climb through the hole into a tunnel, which led us under the bathroom sink and allowed us to exit into the bathroom.

We would roam the house together, taking turns keeping watch by the window. One sister explored the cupboard for a snack. The other sister would hit play on the radio and start dancing. Sometimes we were just happy to go to the bathroom. We never did anything snoopy or dangerous; we were just excited to be out of our room.

Everything was magical until one day when I discovered the consequences of being a gumball glutton.

Our grandparents from my father's side smothered us in love and sugar, as all good grandparents do. One year they got us a penny gumball machine. It was so shiny, with a red top, a glass ball, and a red bottom. They filled the inside with colorful balls of sugary goodness that wouldn't keep the flavor long, so of course, you had to eat many at once. It sat in the living room on a wicker shelf, begging for pennies.

After a long period of not finding pennies, I discovered I could get to the gum by unscrewing the top.

When they presented us with this gift, they were excited, we were excited, and Dad was angry. He didn't think we deserved to have nice things.

On a day like any other, my father locked us in our room and left. We disassembled the dresser and crawled out of our space to roam. But this time, he came back sooner. I sounded the alarm from the window. The girls stopped what they were doing and ran back into the bathroom hole. I was sad because there was no time to get my daily gumball!

They called my name, pleading for me to return to our room.

I just wanted one piece of gum.

I ran from the window to the dispenser and started twisting the top. I angled my arm into the glass bowl. My fingers stretched for the balls of deliciousness as I ignored my sisters' pleas. My fingers touched the tip of a gumball. I just had to reach a little further.

The front door swung open. In an instant, I knew I was in big trouble. The shock in my father's eyes was quickly replaced with a darkness that paralyzed me. Before I could react, he was at my side, lifting me by my arm, yelling and dragging me to our bedroom door, demanding to know how I got out. I didn't answer him. I just squealed, squeaked, and made every noise other than the one he wanted to hear.

He unlocked our door, opened it, and tossed me in the corner next to my sisters. They had reassembled the getaway passage, but the jig was up. As he stood in the doorway, yelling and threatening us, none of us would reveal how we got out. We tried to convince him the door was not locked, but he wasn't buying our story. He threatened a whoopin', but we still wouldn't speak.

Us three girls sat there, huddled on the mattress, still as statues, while spit flung from his mouth. He grabbed my sister by her arm and lifted his hand high with her in it. She screamed, and I couldn't handle the emotion I felt. I blurted out our escape route. My sisters shot daggers at me with their eyes, but I didn't care. I couldn't stand the sound of my sister's cries.

He tipped the dresser revealing our tunnel to freedom. Bewilderment morphed his face for just a second. It was almost as if he was angry that we had the nerve to do what we did.

"You think you are so smart."

After our whoopin', he boarded up the wall, smiled in satisfaction, locked us back in the room, and left again.

MY SISTERS AND I were put into our room most of the day or told to leave the house. We never shared with anyone what was happening at home. We didn't know any different; this was normal to us.

During this particular evening, my sisters were not home. My mother sweetly asked me to stay in my room. She wore a big smile on her face and said it wouldn't be for long. This request was unusual for her as she didn't mind our company. She had never locked us in our room, and I do not know if she knew my father was a repeat offender.

I don't know much about that night, just that my mother let out an ear-shattering scream while I was in my room playing with my Barrel of Monkeys. I felt terror in my gut and ran to my door. My short arms reached up to grasp the knob, twist it, and swing it open just in time to see my mother running down the hall to her bedroom. Her brown curly hair moved across her back as she ran. She was terrified, and I could feel it.

Before stepping out, my father flew past my door and was on her heels. His deep voice echoed in the halls. I could not make out what he was saying or what she was saying, or maybe I don't remember. Either way, none of it was good.

She shut their bedroom door quickly to lock my father out. He punched a hole through the door and reached in to unlock the handle. My mother screamed the entire time. I don't know if my screams, my mother's, or my father's got the police to our home so fast. I watched them rush in behind my father, who had pinned my mother to the bed and was hurting her.

The cops grabbed him under his arms and around his waist to pull him back. They handcuffed and hauled him out of our trailer, putting him in the back of a squad car. The blue and red lights cut through the night as they flashed over my father's face, exposing the anger that still twisted and contorted his once gentle features.

My eyes, once again, took in the lights, cars, and neighbors. My mother was outside now. Her hysteria, shock, and tears engulfed her entire being as she rambled incoherently to the cops. Apparently, another man was in the house with her, but I had never seen him. I overheard them say the other man in our home was the reason for my father's rage.

The cops took statements from anyone who wanted to talk. I watched my mother staring at my father in the cop car as if she feared he would crawl right out of the back seat and chase her again.

Once she calmed down, I noticed she changed to carefully choosing her words to the officers. Even in the hysteria, she had left details about our life out of her answers. She feared him. This fear passed into me, and I, too, scripted my words when speaking to the police.

I'm sure the night was long, but it was over in a flash. The police took my father to jail. Soon the street was void of police cars, the ambulance, fire trucks, and neighbors. Silence blanketed the chaos of that evening, but peace would never enter our home again.

Chapter 6

Not one thing in my life was the same after the police arrested my father that evening.

The divorce battle kicked off thick with hate between my parents. Because of the violence in our home, my father was not allowed custody of me during the trial. The police ordered him not to contact my mother or me. However, they allowed him to live across the street from our trailer. My sisters stayed with other families and were even in foster care for some time.

I watched my mother fluctuate quickly through her emotions. Some days she did not want the restraining order; on others, she enforced it. She would often pace back and forth, looking out the window at the neighbor's house across the street where my father resided. When she wasn't walking back and forth, she would sit on our shoes in the closet with the door closed and cry.

On the days she would cry in the closet, I would sit outside the door and cry with her. One day, I couldn't pretend I didn't know she was in there, and I opened the door, exposing her to the light. I startled her. I crawled onto her lap and sat crying in the closet with her. She would not stop apologizing, not for anything in particular, just sobs of sorry.

I was confused and sad. I missed my sisters. I didn't understand why they couldn't be with us, and although my father had developed a short fuse, I missed him as well.

Something happened one morning. My mother shifted from what I perceived as feeling anguish to being afraid. She kept pacing in our home, her head tilted toward the floor, speaking incoherently under her breath. She bent down and instructed me to run to the neighbor's house to see my father. She had the idea everything would be over if he could see me. She had convinced herself if he laid eyes on me, he would love us again, and we would be a family.

I was hesitant because I could feel her fear. To get me to cooperate, she turned her idea into an adventure. I adored games, and there was always something exciting about being sneaky. Could I make it across the street without anyone noticing? Let's find out.

We peeked out our door to make sure no neighbors were outside, and I booked it barefoot across the gravel road to the trailer. By the short time I arrived on the deck, I was excited. I thought I had won as I looked for any neighbors and saw no one.

I knocked on the flimsy screen door. The loud noise of the rattling door scared me. I looked back at my mother and shrugged my shoulders. She waved her arms about, gesturing for me to try again. I knocked on the door a little louder. The fun of the adventure quickly dissipated and was replaced with hesitation once more.

The door swung open to reveal my father had been sleeping, as he was still in his underwear. One hand held open the inner door, and the other tried to rub the sunlight from his eyes. He looked down at me and, in an instant, was wide awake. He swung open the screen door and pulled me into the home. It was dark. The shades that covered the window facing our trailer were closed.

"What are you doing here? You are not supposed to be here. She knows this!" he said through fierce anger. Now HE was pacing back and forth, speaking under his breath. He thought she was setting him up. If he had any contact with us, he would return to jail.

Maybe she was setting him up. I didn't know. As I stood in the dark living room, looking up at him, I did know one thing. I knew our family was not getting back together as she had hoped.

He knelt and told me I was not supposed to be there and needed to go home. I quickly hurried back to let my mother know he was not happy.

I was not privy to the details of the many court appearances, but like any other child, my ears were always open. When my mother was on the phone, I picked up on a sentence or two. I didn't learn much, other than "he wasn't playing fair," whatever that meant.

I am not sure how much time passed before this change, but one day my mother moved out of the trailer without me, and my father moved in. The courts had decided he was the more fit parent during the rest of the trial and that it was his home. He agreed in court to let my mother see me on the weekends as long as she followed *his* rules.

She was not able to keep a stable home. When I was with her, it was always in a new "better" apartment with a new "better" man, and it was never close in proximity to the home we once shared. My father had moved on as well. There was a new, beautiful woman living back at his house.

My mother still did not have my sisters living with her. She said she needed time to get back on her feet. She would show me pictures of my sisters, but I could not see them or talk to them. I did not understand why. She would distract me with my favorite dinner if I asked too many questions. We ate a lot of mac and cheese with hot dogs and talked about how great the future would be.

I felt like I was the rope in a game of tug-of-war. My father gave my mother a list of rules when I was allowed to see her. Each time I was back home, my father would debrief me. I always felt uncomfortable with the questions my father would ask. I answered them as best as possible, knowing that "I don't know" was not an acceptable answer.

HERE ARE SOME MEMORIES of my time spent during the custody battle and a little after. I was five to six years old.

One night my mother somehow got the band back together, my sisters and I under the same roof. The four of us had not been together for a very long time. We were excited to see each other and spend time with Mom. But our mother had other plans that evening.

It was dark outside, and we were huddled on dirty sheets for a bed on the living room floor. Our mother had put us there and told us to lie down. We had just arrived shortly before, so we'd spent no time with our mother.

The living room had no TV or furniture. It smelled musty,

and the carpet was thick with dirt and whatever else fell onto it. My sisters whispered back and forth. Whenever I would ask what they were talking about, they would tell me I was too young to understand.

My mother went outside to smoke with a group of people. I wasn't supposed to get up, but I wanted to see her, so I peeked out of the dingy window. I had felt everything was going to be okay now that we were all together. "Together, we could do anything." Remember? The feeling of hope dissipated as the clock ticked away in the background, and she showed no signs of coming back in.

After what felt like an eternity, my mother came into the living room. She seemed excited, so we girls started to get excited. We all stood up and surrounded her, speaking at once.

Breathlessly, she told us she would be right back, and we were to go to bed. Realizing her energy was not directed toward us, all of our young voices jumbled together once again as we spat out objections.

"Bed!? But we just got here!"

"Shush," she said. "Now lay down. We have all day tomorrow."

My sisters obeyed. I didn't move.

"Niki, lay down," my mother said.

"But I don't want to lay down, and I'm not even tired. You said we were going to play games," I replied.

Her voice shifted from excitement to impatience as she instructed me again to lie down, adding that I was not to get up. I was back at the window as soon as she was out of the room.

She told us she was going back outside to hang out with her friends, but I watched her from behind the dirty glass.

I watched as she slid into the passenger side of a car. Panic surged throughout my body. I screamed and ran out of the house as the car pulled out of the driveway. My sisters were fast on my heels, unsure of what was happening at first.

I do not know if the others outside hailed the car down. Maybe the driver saw me running down the road. Either way, the vehicle stopped in the middle of the street. My mother got out of the car and ran to me.

"You said you were just going outside. Why are you leaving?" I asked, followed up with more whimpers.

My mom tried to console me. Her hands rested on my shoulders and held me steady. The people standing outside watched the scene unfold. It reminded me of our neighbors when our house burned to the ground and when my parents fought. People always seemed to be watching us.

Suddenly, new energy emerged from my sisters. I was too young to understand, but my sisters were not. My older sister had reached a stage of resentfulness at eight years of age, and that night she confronted our mother.

"Every time you get us, you leave to get high with your friends," she spat out.

Our middle sister tried to comfort the eldest, peeking back at our mother to ensure she was doing the right thing. My jaw hung heavy as I watched my sister yell at our mother.

My mother grabbed my sister's arm and directed her back into the house. My other sister and I followed. "It's bedtime. Now you girls are going to sleep, and we will talk about this in the morning."

We were back on the floor. The air was thick, wet even, so none of us wanted the sheet provided for us to cover up. After I heard the door shut, I tried to get back up to watch again to see if she would leave, but my sisters wouldn't let me. Likely for fear I would get us in further trouble.

"Forget about her. She doesn't care about us," my older sister said.

I lay on the damp carpet in the dark, mulling over her words. *Was it true?* I asked myself. *Did Mom really not care about us? How come she is never around?* Eventually, I fell asleep. That was the last night I remember us girls all under the same roof.

MY MOTHER HAD MET A MAN and moved into his apartment. I am not sure what town it was in, but I remember the car ride was long. He seemed nice and had a couple of kids of his own. He had their pictures on the fridge and showed them to me as he talked about how much he loved them, but he couldn't see them. There was also a picture of me on the fridge with my sisters. They were not living with my mom, and there was no phone for me to call and talk to them.

Mom seemed happy, though. The man never asked me to call him dad, but he was caring toward me. "They were going to be together forever," they'd said. I had only seen him that one time.

One day, my mother needed to make a call. Back then, they didn't have cell phones, and some people didn't even have landlines. Her new boyfriend was one of those people. My mother and I walked down their apartment's long, wooden, unstable stairs and across the street to the bar. I panicked mid-street.

"You are not supposed to take me into a bar!"

During one of my debriefings with my father, he informed me she would never see me again if she took me to a bar.

She knew how serious he was. I couldn't believe she was willing to risk it.

"I know, Niki, but he will never know if you don't tell him. I am not getting a drink. I just need to use the phone to make a quick call," she replied.

"But he will! HE always finds out!" I cried. She hushed me and held my hand tightly, guiding me to the open door of the bar.

She had not lied to me. We were not there long. She made a phone call, kept me at her side the entire time, and then we left. As we crossed the street back to the apartment, I saw my dad at the end of the street. "There's Dad," I said and pointed down the road.

"What?" she replied and looked to where I was pointing, but he was gone.

She didn't believe that I had seen my father. "He wouldn't drive all day just to spy on us," she retorted. But I was sure I had seen him.

Later in one of the custody trials, that very day came into question, or so she said. She asked if I had told my father because, on their next court date, he accused her of bringing me into that bar. He even had pictures. He showed the photos to the judge and said she had been drinking, which put my life in danger.

I was already beginning to see the patterns in our family dynamic and was angry my mother seemed ignorant. It was as if she tried to make him angry.

When she told me of their day in court, I shook my head back and forth.

"I told you he was there," I replied somberly.

MY FATHER DID GAIN full custody of me, but he promised
to let my mother and I see each other. As time went on, my
visits with my mother decreased. I often heard my mother
and father fighting through the cream-colored phone that
hung from the wall with a cord that could stretch across the
kitchen. She seemed to be angry and yet pleading on the
other line. Most of the time, she did not win the argument,
and it ended with him saying something like, "Too bad. No,
never. Not." But sometimes, he would break down and allow
her to take me for the weekend.

When I spent time with my mother, it was never in a nice
home or sleeping in a warm bed. The people my mother
hung out with seemed to be struggling. Their homes were
unkept—foundations crumbling, mold on the walls, cracks
in the floor, boarded windows. No one ever seemed to have
food, and smoke always hung in the air.

MY MOTHER WOULD OFTEN attempt to trick me when
she was going to leave me behind. She would try to sneak
out after distracting me with toys or food. Occasionally it
worked; most of the time, it didn't. When she had custody
of me for the weekend, she would leave me with someone
I had never met. There were times I doubted she knew who
they were.

"But I'm hungry," I whined into her shoulder one night.
I did not know if I was hungry or trying to come up with a
reason to make her stay.

"I know, but there is nothing I can do about that. I do not
have any money right now."

She was leaning down on one knee, her other leg propped
up to steady herself. Her hands had moved to my shoulders

to push me back so I would be face-to-face with her.

"I need to go. You are going to stay here."

I looked around the space we were occupying. We were in a hallway near a washer and dryer that may or may not have been working. Dirty clothes, kitty litter, and worn toys saturated the floor. The home smelled of cat pee and cigarettes. A lady was standing at the round kitchen table with her eyes fixed on us. She had fuzzy, wavy hair tangled and knotted on her shoulders and a cigarette wedged between her pointer and middle finger. Behind her were a few men who focused their attention on my mother and me. Every one of them looked irritated.

"I can't afford to feed her," the lady abruptly clarified. I looked up at her, with her worn clothing hanging loosely on her plump body.

"You don't have to worry about her. She is fine," my mother said as she stood up. They began arguing loudly about something I couldn't understand. I slowly backed up toward the room my mother asked me to stay in, keeping my eyes on my mother and the angry woman. I knew my mother was not going to take me with her. She never did.

My mother flung her hands into the air. "I'll be right back! Just wait," she yelled at the mean lady. My mother took the loitering people with her, leaving the abrasive woman and me to stare at each other. The woman looked at me like I was disgusting. I imagine I looked back at her as if she had seven heads.

MY MOTHER WAS DRIVING a car she had borrowed from someone. Laughter and music filled the car. They were both high, on what I didn't know, and they had also been drinking. I sat in the back seat, watching the hills go by while the sun and wind danced on my face. It was a beautiful day.

A cop car appeared out of nowhere, and his lights and siren quickly made us panic.

My mother told me to put my seat belt on. When the cop came to the window, he asked her why her seatbelt wasn't attached. She told him she took it off after pulling over because she had to reach into the back seat for her purse—a lie.

Lots of bantering back and forth ensued. My mom was pleading, the man in the passenger seat was defending, then my mother told the passenger to shut up. My head darted back and forth to each of their faces as I tried to keep up.

Then the cop looked at me and asked, "Was she wearing her seat belt?" Eyes wide, I froze. I sunk back into the seat as far as I could go. I knew my mother wanted me to lie because she instructed me to do so with pleading eyes.

I couldn't lie. I wouldn't speak, but I bet my face said a lot. After what felt like a lifetime, the cop thanked me for not lying and gave my mother a warning after telling her to do better because her daughter was in the back seat.

I thought my mother would whip around and scold me for not having her back. Instead, she told me she was proud I didn't lie for her and was sorry she put me in that position. My mother was no saint, but she was not the devil either.

I BELIEVE WE WERE somewhere in the country. It may have been right out of town for all I know, but there were no other homes around us and no bathroom in the house we were at.

It was dark outside, but I was not as tired as my mother thought I should be. She told me it was time to lie on the couch and sleep.

"But I'm not tired," I whined. I was upset that I hadn't seen my mother all day, and now that we were together, she wanted me to go to sleep, which was a pattern whenever I visited her.

I looked at the VHS clock showing the night was still early.

I was supposed to stay on the couch to fall asleep, but I was bored, so I kept sneaking around the corner to watch my mother.

She was sitting at the table with a man I had never met. The wooden table was round and lit by a prominent gold fixture on the ceiling. Smoke was exiting her lungs, and she laughed at whatever they discussed.

"Get back on the couch and go to sleep," my mom's voice carried into the living room, startling me.

"What's that smell?" I asked.

"What smell" my mom shot back with fake ignorance.

"That smell. I know you can smell it!" I replied.

Before my mother could respond, the weird man said, "It's skunks. You're out in the country now. Better get used to it."

"How many skunks are out there?" I asked.

"Niki, go to sleep," my mother exhaled.

"But I have to go potty."

"You don't want to go outside when it's dark," said the odd man at the kitchen table.

"But I really have to go!"

"Then head outside," he replied.

"That's not funny."

I thought he was kidding. My mother chuckled at my reaction.

"Look out that window," said the strange man.

I stared him down. I didn't like him and didn't want to turn my back on him. My body turned slowly toward the couch while my eyes stayed on him. My hands guided the way as I climbed onto the end of the sofa and turned my head to press my nose against the cool window.

"You see that shack out there?" he asked. I didn't know what a shack was, but I nodded slowly as my eyes searched.

"Well, then get on out there. If you see anything, run. Don't bother looking for the light; there isn't one." He laughed under his breath, but he was serious. Somewhere in the darkness was a box I was supposed to pee in.

I walked to the back door and stepped outside. I had known it was dark, but it seemed to devour me. I wasn't wearing shoes. The earth felt soft and cool. I stepped carefully, straining my ears to hear anything move in the dark. My feet were ready to dart at any sign of nightlife.

I looked back at the house with the kitchen light streaming out of the living room window and then looked forward toward the outhouse. Its house-like silhouette was dark, but I could still see that it was worn and made of wood. The door was crooked and partially open, with a blue half-moon nailed to the front. I creaked open the door to see inside. Blackness, combined with an awful stench, greeted my face. How badly do I have to go? I asked myself.

I lifted my foot to step into the musty box. The floor was wood, uneven, and moist. I moved in and out of the box to find something to prop open the door. Come on. There has to be something to hold this door open. Maybe I could just pee outside of the box.

"Hurry up," my mother shouted, startling me out of my thoughts. She was standing half in the house, half out, lit by the outdoor light bulb above her head.

"I can't see. I'm scared," I yelled back at her, but she was already gone.

With my hand holding open the "bathroom" door, I looked back into the outhouse. I could see a little better now that my eyes were adjusting to the dark. The toilet seat was chest high. I couldn't just turn around and plop my tush on it; I had to climb up.

I climbed up slowly, trying to ignore my fear warning of spiders, and quickly pulled down my pants. I squatted over the hole and let go of whatever was in my bladder. I am not sure I finished peeing when I pulled up my pants and launched myself out of the standing coffin.

I ran back toward the house and swung open the back door. "Ok, now go to sleep," my mother said.

"And you better not have peed on my seat," said the man at the table without looking at me. I wandered back toward the couch, slightly proud because I was pretty sure I had peed all over his seat, and I felt he deserved that.

I eventually drifted off to sleep by the window to the sounds of the night and the smell of skunks.

Chapter 7

"I love to see a young girl go out and grab the world by the lapels. Life's a bitch. You've got to go out and kick ass."

—MAYA ANGELOU

S ome of my favorite memories are those on a tobacco farm my mother worked at for a summer. To a young tomboy around six years old, the sight of a farm first thing in the morning promised adventure.

In one direction, many heads moved through endless rows of green plants as people picked and tended tobacco leaves. A small black, battery-operated boom box was propped up in the dirt, echoing out tunes to help pass the time. Occasionally, I'd see someone light up a cigarette and complain about the sun's heat.

In the opposite direction was a world filled with unpleasant, overpowering aromas. Fences cornered in the surrounding dirt, manure, goats, cows, and the like. A large hay barn, which I was not supposed to explore, was at the far end. The animals paid no attention to me as I lay on my back, sliding in and out of their pens.

"Stay close!" I would hear my mother yell. I would turn back and wave to let her know I heard her, intending to listen. My mother would work for hours, and I would roam the farm, climbing under electric fences, over wooded ones, and creating a new adventurous reality.

I wasn't supposed to go into the hay barn because it was dangerous. The hay bales were stacked on each other, creating a giant fun mountain. I could have fallen down the stacks or through them, but that wasn't the real danger, although it could have been if no one had noticed.

My mother asked me to steer clear because of the large tractor stacking large bales inside the barn. One tire alone was taller than some cars.

I thought my curiosity could be satisfied if I peeked in the door. I wanted to see for myself the tallest king of the mountain challenge. The mountain of straw seemed to reach the sky. The allure was overwhelming. My legs started moving toward the highest hay peak I had ever seen. Gigantic tire tracks molded the soil covering the barn floor. The little voice in my head warned me, *I shouldn't be in here*.

I climbed those bales better than Spiderman. I was jumping and rolling at the top of the hay when a loud machine, getting louder, caught my attention. Through the cracks in the barn wall, I could see the tractor heading back to the barn. The tires crunched over the dirt and rocks. I panicked. I rolled down the mountain and ran toward the open door as fast as I could.

I was too late.

Now a tiny body sandwich, I was stuck between the hay bales and the giant black tires heading in my direction. I stopped and looked up at the massive machine coming my way.

A worker, who had been dating my mom for a short time, was driving the tractor. He stopped the loud machine just a few feet from where I stood, eyes up, jaw on the floor. He tossed the door open, jumped, landed hard, and sprinted toward me. He grabbed me by my arm and started to yell. The fear of facing down the tractor still had my adrenaline pumping, making it difficult to focus on what he was saying.

He tried to pull me toward him to give me a whoopin', but I reached out to the tractor and held on tight to a tractor handle. He could not pull me closer without ripping my arm out of its socket. I was terrified and began to scream as if someone were tearing me apart.

He realized something wasn't right. He let go of me and watched as I continued to scream. Realizing he had let go, I looked back at him over my shoulder. His face creased into a frown, his head pulled back as his eyes narrowed, and his arms fell to his side. I wasn't acting like a normal kid afraid to get a whoopin'. I was hysterical.

He stepped back and continued to observe me. He crouched on a knee.

"Niki, come here," he said in a soft voice. His arms were outstretched. I sniffled, watching him. I didn't want to trust him, but I could see confusion, fear, and sadness in his eyes, not anger.

"No, you're going to hit me," I said, not trusting myself or him.

"I was going to give you a spanking, but I am not anymore. Come here. I want to talk to you."

"Promise you won't hit me."

"I promise I won't spank you if you come here now."

Hesitantly, I walked over to his arms. As I got closer, I believed he wouldn't hurt me. I fell into his hug, allowing my wet cheek to land on his shoulder.

"I'm sorry. I didn't mean to scare you, but you scared me! That barn is dangerous, and your mother told you! I almost didn't see you. I could have killed you. I overreacted," he sighed.

My eyes filled with tears of relief. He was not going to hit me. *Why does he care for me so much? He barely knows me.* A stranger showed more concern than my father ever had, making me believe even more that my father hated me. *Why else would my father hurt me as he did? Why couldn't my father love me?*

The man pushed my shoulders from himself so he could look me square in the eye. "Promise me I will not catch you in there again."

I promised, and I never went into the barn again. He trusted me, and that was all I needed to keep me from disappointing him.

MY FATHER CAME to pick me up from the tobacco farm. I could hear my parents arguing, but I wasn't paying attention, though everyone else on the farm was. My focus was on a little black boom box singing the words, "I thought that I heard you laughing, I thought that I heard...."

My mother called my name, but I didn't turn around.

She walked over to me, knelt, and took my face in her hands to get my attention. I could see my father behind her watching us, angry as usual. She smiled, told me she loved me and wrapped me in her arms. She was always good at hugs.

I said goodbye to my mother. This may not have been the last time I saw my mother, but it was the last time I remember seeing her.

Chapter 8

"All great changes are preceded by chaos."

—DEEPAK CHOPRA

I discovered later in life my mother was trying to hide my sisters from their father. To do so, she put them in foster care. Their father was looking for them, and it wasn't until our mother tried to get government assistance (even though she did not have us in her custody) that he could find them because the county contacted him.

Wherever my sisters were at this point, someone gave them our home number, and I could finally talk to them on the phone. When the phone would ring, my legs would propel me into the kitchen, yelping with excitement.

One day I heard my father tell them I wasn't there, and he hung up the phone.

The first time I heard this, a whimper escaped my throat as I stared up at my father in disbelief.

"But I am here," I whispered.

"Go back to your room!" he exhaled in frustration.

That incident repeated itself many times.

Every time the phone rang, I would be so excited and

hopeful that I would talk to my family. But it would end with me standing in the kitchen, my jaw dangling and my eyes stretched wide.

One day I mustered enough courage to ask why I couldn't speak to them.

He replied, "They are not your sisters."

He told me I would no longer see my mother, would never see my sisters, and I was to call my new stepmom Mom from that day forward. Any objection to that would be my behind.

One evening I picked up a letter on the kitchen table where my father sat going through the day's mail. My stepmother was at the kitchen counter washing dishes.

I read the name on the envelope aloud—my stepmother's maiden name.

My father's voice cut through the silence.

"Don't you ever say her name! She is your mother. You address her as a mom!"

He launched from the table at me. I fell back, and my bottom hit the floor. I sputtered out apologies and explanations as I crawled backward away from him.

My stepmother interrupted his yelling and pleaded for him to stop. She told him I was only reading the mail, but he turned and snapped at her. The same way he used to yell at my mother.

She stepped back. Her voice caught in her throat. She was not familiar with this side of my father.

I was still sitting on the floor, trying to understand what I had done wrong, when he turned his attention back to me.

"Don't apologize to me! You apologize to her!" he said while pointing his finger at my stepmother.

I looked at my stepmother, who looked back at me,

scared. She started to say something, but one look from him sealed her lips. She looked at me, pleading as if I could control his anger.

I pulled myself up off the floor, walked gingerly around my father, and wrapped my arms around her waist. "I'm sorry," I said.

Once again, his voice cut into the air, causing me to jump.

"Mom! I'm sorry, Mom!" he said.

"I'm sorry, Mom," I repeated.

"Good. Now go to your room." He huffed and sat back down at the table.

My stepmother did not stick up for me much after that, at least not while I was present. A few times, I remember her putting her foot down and not allowing him to control her, but those moments were few and far between as time moved on.

She had my back one night when I was not feeling well. I mentioned it to my father when he called me for dinner. He had made chicken dumpling soup. I sat at the table, feeling my stomach swirl. I kept telling him I did not feel well. His short temper came on like fire. I started to eat the soup, but my stomach turned faster.

My stepmother put her hand on my forehead. "She is warm."

"She is fine!" he snapped back at her. He turned his attention to me. "Eat!"

I tried to eat again. My world started to spin, and I told my parents I would throw up. My father would have none of my pleadings. I vomited in my soup and all over the table. He was so angry he put his hand on the back of my head and pushed it toward the soupy vomit.

"You are going to eat every bite of this!"

Tears covered my cheeks, and whimpers escaped my burning throat as I tried to avoid the vomit.

"Stop!" my stepmother yelled. She snatched me up from under his grasp and took me to the bathroom to clean me up. She left me in the bath and went out to confront him.

"As soon as she gets out here, she is eating this soup!" he yelled.

"No, she is not! That is disgusting. You think she can puke on demand now?" she yelled back.

I heard a clink in the sink as his voice echoed in the house. "What are you doing!?"

"She is not eating this! She is taking a bath and then going to bed!"

After a few more minutes of listening to them argue, I came out of the bath. I went to my father to apologize for not feeling well. He looked disgusted at me and said I was lucky she was there. At that time, I was glad she was there too.

Chapter 9

"Courage, sacrifice, determination, commitment, toughness, heart, talent, guts. That is what little girls are made of."

—BETHANY HAMILTON

I had told the teachers many times about this boy who was mean to me. I also spoke to my parents, and no one took me seriously. My school had some mean kids, but this kid was dreadful. He told me my parents hated me, and my sisters left because they couldn't stand me.

When I shared my struggles, the teachers said things like, "He must like you," and "I'm sure he's a sweet kid who doesn't mean anything by it." (Side note: Don't teach your young girls that an asshole is being an asshole because he likes you. Not setting healthy future relationship boundaries.)

Every day I would walk home from school while he walked a few feet in front of me. He spent the whole walk spinning back around and telling me some new hate line he'd cooked up that he couldn't wait to feed me.

One day, I was so frustrated and overwhelmed I was crying. My tears seemed to fuel him further. He laughed and kicked up his heels in dance as he realized he had finally broken me. Then something changed inside me.

I felt a heat rise in my body and spread across my chest. My stomach felt empty, but at the same time, it felt solid. My breath slowed down as my heart sped up. Darkness swept through my body, and I let it. I'd had it with this kid.

We were almost to my house when I devised a plan to scare this boy into leaving me alone. I picked up one of the dusty-red bricks from behind our pitched-up metal shed. I allowed the darkness that was taking over to seep out of my eyes as I told him through tight lips that if he didn't leave me alone, I would kill him and his mother while they slept. My words were graphic as I spoke my empty threats carefully and with an eerie calmness like I had seen my father do.

His eyes grew wide. I could see the fear in him for the first time. "You're crazy!" he yelled, with a few other choice words. He spun around and took off, running home.

And scene.

I was pleasantly surprised my plan had worked. I figured I wouldn't have to deal with my bully anymore. I never thought he liked me, but if he did, he certainly didn't now. I dropped the brick back into place, dusted the powder from my hands, and continued home. I was happy that it was finally over.

It wasn't over. He told his mother, who called the cops. They came to our house while I was away and told my stepmother what I had done. Later that evening, I returned home. My father was at work, and my stepmother was a little more than upset.

After a few verbal lashings, my stepmother said the cops would be back to talk to me. They never did follow-up. I'm sure they didn't believe a young girl would be capable of such hatred. From where would she have learned such violence?

Maybe the officer told the boy I said those mean things because I liked him.

My bully was not to contact me, but he picked up right where he left off in his bully bible, and no one stopped him.

After my stepmother expressed her mortification that I was her daughter and I had brought the police into her home, she put on The Little Mermaid movie. The Little Mermaid was my all-time favorite. I was fascinated with Ariel's sense of adventure, free spirit, and beauty. I could recite each line word for word of the Disney version.

Maybe you didn't know there was another story. They start similarly.

The Little Mermaid I am referring to is the fairy tale told by Hans Christian Andersen in 1836, originating in Denmark. In 1975, a Japanese anime film was produced based on Hans' fairy tale. He was known to be one of the best storytellers of his time.

It starts with Princess Marina (the little mermaid) swimming through the ocean with her dolphin friend Fritz. A storm begins brewing as they introduce the sea witch, sending Marina to race home.

Marina's adventures led her to see her prince on a ship under the stars for the first time. She watched him on the ship and fell in love. The sea witch started a storm to bring down another of the prince's ships, this time with the prince on it! She found her prince in the ocean and wrapped her arms around his unconscious body, swimming him to dry land. Early the next morning, a group of women walked onto the beach. Marina had no choice but to flee. Her prince woke up to another woman, who he believed had saved him.

Marina decides she can't live without the prince, so she

goes to the sea witch, hoping she can say a spell that will turn her human. Fritz does everything he can to stop her, but as the sea witch explains, "It's true love that makes us blind." Once she has received her human legs, the sea witch tells her she will never be a mermaid again. If she cannot win the prince's love, her heart will break the morning he is wed to another, and she will turn to foam on the waves.

The prince finds Marina on the beach the next morning, with no clothing, unable to speak, and takes her back to the castle. The prince has an arranged marriage. This arrangement concerns the prince. He wants to marry the girl he thinks saved his life. But he doesn't believe he can find her, so the prince decides he wants to marry Princess Marina.

But his parents trick him, and they take away his princess Marina. They force the prince to meet the other princess they have arranged for him. The prince is pleased as he discovers the princess is the one he thinks saved his life. They announce their marriage right away.

At the movie's end, Marina is on the ship's deck while her prince is in bed with his new wife. Her sisters' voices interrupt her thoughts, and she looks at the sea to find them. They tell her that she can return to the sea if she kills the prince. The witch gave them a dagger. Marina has to plunge the knife into the prince's heart. Her legs will become a tail when his blood spills to her feet.

The princess walks down to the room where her prince and his new wife lay asleep. She walks silently to his bedside, lifting the dagger above his heart. The music intensifies. Marina drops to her knees, unable to kill her first love. She returns to the ship's top deck and drops the dagger into the sea. When the dagger hits the water, the prince wakes up and runs to the deck. He calls to her, but with tears in her eyes, she jumps off the back of the ship, committing suicide.

She floats in the water. Bubbles surround her until she is dead and part of the sea forever. At this moment, the spell breaks, and the prince remembers who Marina was and that she was the one who saved him. His eyes fill with tears as he realizes what he has lost.

The story ends with the piercing cries of her best friend, Fritz.

Though the crying in the movie had stopped, my wails of pain cut through the silence. Tears flooded my face as I ran to my stepmother, who was in front of the washer doing laundry. At first concerned, she asked what was wrong. Between sobs and heaves, I managed to get out that Marina had killed herself.

She stepped back and told me to grow up.

"Why are you so upset? Remember what you said to that boy earlier? Someone with a heart would not have said that, so I don't understand why you are so upset about a stupid movie."

I stared up at her in disbelief. "You don't think I have a heart!? I told you that boy was mean to me!" I cried out. I slumped back to my room and sobbed on the floor.

Marina's pain was too much for her to bear. For Princess Marina, death was the only way out. I had thought about how little I could see my mother, how I hadn't seen my sisters and the daily ritual of my bully's antics. I thought about how hard it was to sit still in school and why I was so bad that my father and my new mother hated me. After all those thoughts, a final one entered my mind, *Should I give up too? Is this my only way out?*

Chapter 10

"Courage doesn't always roar. Sometimes courage is the quiet voice at the end of the day saying, 'I will try again tomorrow.'"

—MARY ANNE RADMACHER

learned at a young age I could tell what kind of day I would have by the sound of my father's voice. When he yelled, I knew to stay out of his way. It would be a tense day, but I could spend most of it hiding outside. If he called sweetly to me, the day would be worse.

When he called out in his soft voice, something in his tone made me hesitant and untrusting. It was like he was my friend, but he did not have a history of being friendly.

I started becoming more afraid when we were alone in the house. I could be watching TV or playing in my room when he would ask me a seemingly innocent question. At first, I didn't think much of his new friendly behavior. I was happy he talked nicely to me. I thought he finally loved me, and maybe things were getting better. Perhaps I was doing something right.

After a while of this new dynamic, he started asking unusual questions that were more like puzzles. His most commonly used mind trick was to ask, "Would you like a hot dog?" Sometimes he would say a wiener, or a popsicle, at the time, some of my favorite foods. This phrase would lead me to think we were talking about lunch. I would say yes to the lunch offer, and he would tell me to go into the bedroom or the bathroom.

That he was talking about lunch but not about lunch baffled me. He would tell me I could have a hot dog but couldn't bite it. Or that I could have a popsicle, but it wouldn't be cold. It did not take long to catch on to the fact that I was not getting food.

Recanting my yes and casually saying I was not hungry would not deter my father's plans. My next attempt was to outwit him, but he would get sick of my stalling and change his approach back to anger. "You said you wanted a hot dog; now you are going to get one. If you don't eat it now, you are not getting one later," he would say as if we were still talking about food.

My earliest memory of these moments was when I was about five years old. Once my father would get me into the bedroom, he would instruct me to remove my clothes and blindfold me with the belt of his robe. I could feel the soft strap around my eyes and the tension as he tightened the knot behind my head. He would lift me into the air as if I weighed nothing and lay me on the bed. The knot would dig into the back of my skull while I squirmed on the sheets, anxious to get away from him.

With my clothes tossed on the floor, I could feel the cold air on my exposed skin. The smell of the room and his scent felt suffocating. He would hold my legs together, and I could feel him moving on top of me as he rubbed himself on me.

He didn't think I could see with the blindfold, but I could always peek out where my nose lifted the cloth slightly. I can still see the dark hair on his torso, his stomach moving back and forth, and his tongue stuck out in concentration. His heavy breathing would push his breath toward my face.

I felt sick. I would lie on the bed, hoping someone would come home and interrupt whatever was happening. I thought if I wished hard enough, my mother would arrive. My ears strained to hear someone walk in or knock on the door. Instead, all I heard were gasps and moans.

My father's breath smelled rancid, never like alcohol, just spoiled. He once said he didn't like not being in control, so he wouldn't drink much, if ever.

I could feel his rough fingers between my legs as they scraped the tender skin inside me. I tried to slide my hips back up the sheets. Tears dampened the tie around my eyes.

One day, I felt something much bigger than his finger near me. I didn't recognize what it was and panic shook my entire body. Even though the rope blocked any outside light, a light from behind my eyes blinded me as a high-pitched scream escaped. I ripped the blindfold off and screamed louder, fully sitting at this point and scrambling to get away.

"Shhh shhh, it's okay. It's okay. We'll do this instead," he said as he put the blindfold back on my nose. A whimper escaped my throat as my body went limp once again. I was exhausted.

THERE WERE OTHER TIMES when he took me into the bathroom. The scenario always started the same, asking if I was hungry with a soft edge to his voice. I knew what would happen but acted as though I was confused and tried many tactics to avoid the upcoming moment. He would begin by removing all my clothes, blindfolding me, and sitting me on the edge of the cold tub.

My bare bottom felt slippery on the edge of the tub. The room was cold, but the tub was icy. My skin felt clammy, and my thighs were on the tub edge, so my feet couldn't touch the floor. The blindfold was hurting me. My father had once noticed I could see under the belt, so he made the knot tighter to stop it from moving.

He told me to open my mouth wide. He stuck his penis in my mouth and instructed me along the way. I scrunched my nose in this memory, told him it tasted awful and asked to go to my room. He said, "Hang on." I heard the sink water running, so I peeked out from under my blindfold and watched him look down at himself while wiping his penis with a wet rag. I quickly pushed the blindfold back up my nose.

I could hear his steps as he walked back toward me.

"That should be better," he said as he stuck his member in my mouth again.

I gagged and repeated that my "hot dog" tasted gross. I thought my whining would give me freedom, but it did not. My father instructed me to lay back on the tub edge, but that didn't allow him the access he wanted, so he picked me up and laid my bare butt on the toilet seat. He instructed me to lean back as he spread my legs. I was unsure how much time had passed before I felt a warm liquid on my stomach and heard his gasp.

He stepped back. My position made my neck and back hurt, and I hated not seeing. I started to squirm on the seat. I began to lift myself from the toilet seat, but he instructed me to stay. I heard him walk over to the sink and was surprised when a wet cloth landed on my belly.

"Clean yourself up," he said and walked out of the bathroom.

I was stunned but glad to be alone. I lifted the blindfold from my eyes and looked at the tub, the toilet I was still sitting on, then into the mirror, back at my naked body.

I knew I needed help but didn't know how to get it. I never told my mother what he was doing. I didn't think I could get help from my stepmother, who also seemed scared of my dad.

I had a friend who I played with often. One night we were in her backyard fort when I told her, "My father is having sex with me." She asked more questions, and I answered them. Looking back, I am amazed at how brave she was. She immediately told me what he was doing was wrong. Her anger was so aggressive I felt embarrassment, fear, and panic and yelled out a defense for my father.

"No, he would never hurt me. He loves me," I said. Even as I defended him, I felt that sickness.

She replied, "My father would never do that because he loves me."

"But you won't tell anyone, right?"

"You have to tell someone!"

"No! I can't tell anyone! Please, you have to keep your mouth shut!"

"Okay fine. Let's go inside. I'm hungry."

My friend and I climbed down from her fort and walked into her house. Her father was in their living room watching TV.

"Tell him!" she quickly said, her voice high enough to catch her father's attention, and she blocked the door so I couldn't turn back. I stared back at her, speechless.

"I trusted you!"

"Tell me what?" he said.

"You said you wouldn't tell!"

"Tell me what?"

I turned to him slowly and whispered the same information I had told his daughter. He didn't say anything for a moment. He just looked at me wide-eyed. Then he was angry. I panicked again and tried to defend my father. If I could only get them to understand that he loved me!

My friend's father would have none of my defense as he told me a real man would never do that to his child. My shoulders fell from the weight of my shame and fear. Her father called the school, and he called the cops. He filed a report to have my father investigated.

The police came to my home. I tried answering their questions, but I felt intimidated because they spoke to me like I had done something wrong. They sat at our table and leaned in toward me, almost hovering, while my father watched me a few feet away with his arms crossed.

His eyes burned my skin while I focused on the condescending cop before me. The officer kept repeating if I didn't take back what I said, they would have to take me away from my family.

"Surely you do not understand what sex is, and IF this is true, it will get your father in real trouble. We will have to take you away from your family. Is that what you want?"

Did I understand what sex was? Was I confused? Was what he was doing normal?

I started to second-guess myself, and the hovering cop didn't seem like he was going to be much help. My confidence deflated, and I took it all back. No one thought anything of it either. No one wanted to know why I would have said all those things. They just figured their job was done and left.

The cops left, and nothing changed in our home except that I could not hang out with my friend or anyone else. I had to switch schools again, and my father punished me for "lying."

Although my friend's father's attempts didn't get far, what he did for me was show me real courage. He tried to help me, but the system wouldn't support it.

THE ABUSE CONTINUED and morphed into something incomprehensible to me. One of my most vivid memories is cleaning the kitchen floor. My father instructed me to remove all of my clothes. I stood in the kitchen, looking at my clothes piled against the wall. My father handed me a toothbrush and a bucket filled with soap.

"I want to be able to eat off it."

He stepped back and watched me scrub the kitchen floor with my toothbrush and my derriere high in the sky.

"Higher. Scrub faster. You like this, don't you? Why are you crying?" He spoke in a mocking tone.

I was around six years old and felt humiliated, scared, sad, and confused. I will never forget the way he looked at me while I cleaned. I could not understand why he would be so happy hurting me.

One day, I cried out between tight lips while still on the floor, toothbrush in hand.

"Why are you doing this to me!?"

"All you are doing is scrubbing the floor. Is this too much for you? Do you need a nap? Does baby need a nap?"

He acted as though I was crazy for not wanting to clean

the floor this way. He worked as though he was doing me a favor, and I did not appreciate him.

At the time, I felt life couldn't get worse, but as he often reminded me, I was wrong.

Chapter 11

"Fear is the main source of superstition and one of the main sources of cruelty. To conquer fear is the beginning of wisdom."

—BERTRAND RUSSELL

On the summer days, I would skip lunch and dinner if it meant I didn't have to go home. I spent as much time outside as I could. I liked playing with boys more than girls. The girls were straight-up vicious. Some of the tomboys would try to make friends with me, but I had difficulty making friends.

I once heard a parent call me "that girl." She told me a few minutes later that she did not want her daughter to spend time with someone "like me." I didn't understand what she meant.

The boys and I would toss around the football, sneak under the barbed wire fence into the cow field, and hang out in the eighth graders' tree fort when they weren't looking. We played video games and threw rocks at hornets' nests. Even the nightfall seemed magical as we competed to see who could get the most lightning bugs into a mason jar.

I was already feeling self-conscious as a young girl. Trying to fit in was hard enough, but I faced a new challenge.

I loved my long hair. Playing outside all day caused knots and tangles. My father told me I needed to take care of my hair. He was not taking time to comb my hair, so I am not sure why it bothered him as much as it did, but he decided enough was enough. He brought me to a hairdresser and had her cut off all of my hair into a boy cut. I sat in the waiting room while the hairdresser tried to convince him otherwise, but he would have none of it. That night I left looking like a boy. The next day I was teased by both the girls and the boys.

WHEN SCHOOL STARTED, I struggled. I was "that girl." The worst part was I didn't know what it meant exactly. I did well with group tasks, but sitting still or working independently was hard. I would often disrupt other students and play around to avoid the silence in the room. I felt like my teacher didn't like me much. I gathered this intel on my own after many teachers said, "I can't deal with you anymore. Go to the principal's office."

I was not acting out on purpose. When I felt intimidated or cornered, I would react the same way I did when my father sweetly called my name. I pretended not to hear, saying things that would upset them with the hope I would be left alone, and when all else failed, I starred in a soap opera, which always resulted in me getting into trouble.

When the principal was sick of seeing me in his office, my punishment moved me into the older kids' class, and honestly, I loved it. They were learning cool things that excited me. In one study, they learned how our brains and sense of smell affect our tastebuds. I was so interested in what they were studying that I would sit with a smile. Sometimes, I would raise my hand to answer the question. I started getting in trouble often so that I could join their class. I didn't want to learn how to draw straight lines "because it was an art and important for my future."

One day, I heard the older class teacher tell my teacher, "I don't know what she is doing in your class, but in my class, she is very well-behaved. She even engages in our discussion." My chin lifted high as I swelled with pride. Maybe they would move me to this class, even though they were many classes ahead of me. However, my teacher took offense to this news and told the teacher I was the worst kid in her class. She also informed the teacher that sitting in her class would no longer be my discipline since I enjoyed her teachings. My chest deflated, and from that day forward, I was impatiently disruptive in any classroom they put me in.

The following year, in second grade, I was placed in a private school in another town. The change in scenery did not change my attitude. The only peace I found was sitting in the principal's office. He was a soft-spoken man, and I enjoyed talking to him. I felt safe with him.

There were many private school rules, and one of the musts was drinking milk during lunch. They would have the pouches of white and chocolate milk in the big blue-gray tubs. If you wanted chocolate, you better hustle. I didn't like either, but the chocolate was better than white any day.

Every time I drank it, I would get a stomachache and end up in the bathroom. My teachers thought I was making my pain up. A teacher would sit with me every day at lunch to ensure I finished my milk, so I often missed recess.

One day I blankly refused. I leaned back, crossed my arms, and flat-out said, "No, you can't make me."

Their response to that was to call my father and have him come pick me up for disobeying the teacher.

The school was a little over thirty minutes away from our home. My father came to pick me up. He didn't say anything to me when he arrived, his face stoic. I got in the car and waited for my verbal lashing, but it didn't come. While on the way home, we turned off onto a back road leading to Grandma's house. My body flooded with relief. Finally, he understood the milk was hurting me, and I would see Grandma.

I could not have been more wrong. My father pulled over on the side of the road and told me to get out. I did not move. I stared back at him, confused. We were on a back road with no traffic, no houses, not even a place to park. He was in the middle of the road.

He yelled louder, "Get out!"

I opened the door and stepped out of his car.

"Find a branch."

My mind raced with thoughts of what he was planning, but I had no idea what would come next. I walked from the car, scanning the road for a branch. He leaned back in the car with his arms crossed and watched me search. When I picked my first branch, he said it wasn't good enough.

"Find one bigger."

Hesitant and frightened, I scanned the road for a thicker stick. When I brought my next option to my father, he smiled and asked, "That's the one you want?"

"I guess so?" I replied with little relief. His smile made me feel like he had something fun planned, but I suspected it would not be fun for me.

He instructed me to get into the car. I opened the door and started to put my foot on the floorboard. I was startled when his voice cut through my thoughts. "Not like that."

I placed my foot back outside the car.

"Take off your pants and your underwear."

I stood motionless for a moment.

"Now!"

I scrambled to remove my clothing.

Get in, headfirst," he spoke.

"What do you mean?" I replied.

He got out of the car and slammed his door. Within a few strides, he was right next to me. I was terrified. He grabbed my hair from the back and pushed my head into the floorboard. Simultaneously, using my shirt as a handle, he lifted my legs from outside the car and put my knees on the seat. He squeezed my legs together and put my hands behind my back.

I was not allowed to put my hands on the floor. This position resulted in my bare butt in the air and my body's weight balancing on my head. My neck hurt instantly.

The sound of the door slamming scared me. I could not see anything with my nose on the floor. My ears started to make a whooshing sound as the blood began to pool in my head. I heard his door open and shut again.

My father put the car in gear. He had picked up my chosen stick and began whipping my bare bottom. By his level of force, while hitting, he made me chant along between sobs that I would drink my milk every day. I choked on the words, on my tears, and my screams while he whipped me.

The dirt covering the floor mat scratched at my face as I tried to balance during turns and while he drove over bumps in the road. It took us just under twenty minutes to get home.

Before we pulled up to our home, he told me to put my pants on. "Can't have the neighbors asking questions," he said. I wanted to stick my bare butt against a window while trying to put my undies and pants back on, but I didn't dare defy him.

Chapter 12

"Nothing can stop me from loving my brother."

—BRANDY NORWOOD

In a moment, with a slip of the tongue, I found out I was getting a brother. "Here are the lemon drops. These helped with my pregnancy," my stepmother's sister said.

"You're pregnant!?" I shouted.

My stepmother's sister was unaware my parents did not share the good news with me. My parents stated they were unsure how I would react, so they didn't tell me. Did they think I was never going to find out?

Regardless, I was excited! I was eight years old and had not seen my sisters for years. I missed them. Having a brother to hang out with was going to be great.

I began to have questions during the pregnancy and after. If my stepmother and father were having sex and she got pregnant, did that mean I could too? I didn't want to be pregnant. I didn't know what it meant. I didn't even understand sex, but I knew I didn't want to throw up a lot like her.

One morning, I had been out playing with a neighborhood

boy. I couldn't let go of the fear that I could get pregnant. I started asking the friend I was playing with questions about sex he couldn't answer. He told me I could ask his mother, so we went to his house.

I tried to ask my questions, but I couldn't explain the reason for my concerns. My friend's mother's eyebrows seemed permanently folded together, and she kept digging for information I was not supposed to tell anyone. I ended up getting no closer to the answer I needed.

I went home to my father, working at the front of the trailer. My belly did flip-flops as I thought about how I would ask the question haunting my mind. His sharp voice snapped me out of my thoughts when he asked me what I wanted. I quietly asked him if I could get pregnant like my stepmom. His head whipped back and forth as if looking to see if anyone was around.

"No, that's stupid. Now go on."

My legs were shaking, and my heart was racing, but I had to understand. Could I carry a child? I was barely eight years old. Was that possible? Wouldn't I die?

My mouth started to word-vomit my questions. This interrogation resulted in a furious father and me sprinting away without solid answers.

I asked my stepmother if a kid my age could get pregnant. She said no. I don't think she knew why I was asking. When a child learns about pregnancy, it makes sense to wonder if they, too, could carry a child. One of the most popular toys for young girls is baby dolls.

My brother was such a sweet boy. I picked on him as a bigger sister would, but I loved him in a way I could never describe. We had a bond, just the two of us, which was nice because I didn't feel like I had anyone else.

I thought having a brother would bring our family closer together. However, it became clear I was not part of the new family. Often, I would hear them playing together, and if I asked to join, I would be met by my father's irritated sigh and told to go away.

One evening the sound of my brother's laughter called me out of my room and into the living room. The vacuum cleaner was on. My brother sat in front of my stepmother, his back to her belly. She was sitting in front of my father, between his legs, her back to his stomach. It was a little family train with my brother as the railway engine and my father as the caboose.

My stepmother was vacuuming my brother's hair with the vacuum's hose, causing an explosion of giggles. Immediately excited, I asked if I could join, but my request had ruined the mood. My stepmother's smile turned to worry as she looked at my father. Disgust covered my father's face. "Go back in your room and don't come out unless you are called," he replied.

Most kids feel left out and jealous when more family is born, but I wasn't that kid. I grew up with two older sisters. One of my sisters and I were inseparable—well before my parents separated. So, I was excited to have a brother who loved me just about as much as he loved his airplane swing.

My parents had hung a Little Tikes Red Orange Airplane Rocket Bucket on a beam outside our home. His tiny body sat perfectly as I gently pushed him forward. I was far too big, but he had so much fun it was tempting to try to fit inside.

On Halloween one year, he was Superman. It was a cold year, so he had to wear his Superman outfit under his jacket, and a red hat topped off his look.

He was so cute. My costume was forgotten that year, so my stepmother threw it together at the last minute. I wore an old dress and a funny mask that she found in her closet. My brother could not stop laughing at my face.

He LOVED me.

The years flew, and he grew—a typical boy finding trouble in ordinary ways, but my brother's heart was pure and full of love.

All these years, I have believed he did not know what was happening to me behind closed doors. If he had asked, I never would have told him. I would have wanted to keep his heart pure. I have learned as an adult that we all have stories, and our paths have convinced me he has one too. I guess he couldn't tell me either.

I am not trying to paint a picture of the perfect kid. He could find trouble just as quickly as I did. I picked on him as an older sibling would, though no one else was allowed to pick on him.

One of the kids from our trailer court, a little older than me, which would have made him eight or nine years older than my brother, said some awful things to him one day. My brother went home crying. I was in a rage.

The following day all the trailer court kids gathered to wait for the school bus. That boy who hurt my brother missed the school bus. He was back home with a busted face and a few other bruises.

I made it very apparent to those boys that my brother was off-limits. My love for my brother goes deeper than anything I have ever felt. It's strange how some can easily hurt their family, and others could lose themselves to protect them.

Chapter 13

"Don't worry about fitting in—it's completely overrated."

—NICOLA WALKER

We moved out of our trailer court and into a new city. From one trailer court to another to start a new life. I was getting used to switching homes and schools. Heading into fourth grade, I had already changed schools four times; this would be my fifth.

I was plagued with a curious mind. My parents did not appreciate my constant questions. To them, a question was disobedience. My grandmother understood my eccentric mind and kept it occupied when I was with her. We did puzzles, workbooks, and games, picked wild raspberries, and chased down frogs. As close as we were, I never did drum up the courage to share with her what was happening at home.

The fourth grade started in a new private, Lutheran school.

All the other students had grown up together. They went to church together, on class trips, to everyone's birthday parties, and so forth. They all seemed to get their clothes from the same store—not the one my parents shopped for my clothes. The girls were quiet, clean, and pretty, and these boys did not play with girls. I did not fit in.

I was not helping my case either. I did not make it easy for anyone to be friends with me. There was no point. Although I wanted to be accepted and a part of this tight group, I would never have been able to hang out after school or on weekends. I was not a normal kid, and I figured this out as I grew up.

I was honest, blunt, and curious, but I was not a bully. That whole "kids can be cruel" thing is no joke. But as you get older, you realize that kids are lost, scared, unsure, and insecure, and you let it go. Yeah, the bullies sucked, but I adapted. Putting up with bullies is like a rite of passage. When you grow up, you realize hurt people hurt people, and you feel sorry for that kid who sat on your head, squishing your face into the bus seat. Besides, it was better than what was happening at home.

I learned how to push down my instinct to love and connect with other people. I was a quick student, not in school but in life. Anger kept people at a distance. Outbursts made people uncomfortable. I couldn't get too trusting and expose my secret, so I would disrupt the natural order anytime I felt too safe.

I never had the opportunity to explore who I was. I felt deeply lost. I began to see the worst in people. I learned adults lie. People only like you based on what you can offer them. To be accepted, you must openly judge others, manipulate, scream louder, and cry alone.

Everyone seemed to know more about me than I did, but their judgments were cruel and inappropriate. The only thing left to do was prove them right.

Even if I could have friends, I didn't understand what it

meant to be a good friend. One time a classmate asked me to stay at her house for a few days. She was a popular kid. Right away, I was nervous. My mind came up with many scenarios that did not end well for me.

I was tense most of my stay, but eventually, I relaxed, and we connected. It was as if I had stepped out of my life, my pain, and was living everyday life with a real friend who was intelligent, talented, and beautiful. We could share secrets no one else would know and grow a bond no one could break.

Reality hit when my new "friend" let it slip that she was glad the weekend wasn't awful. She was previously upset because her mother had spoken to my parents, which somehow resulted in her being forced to invite me over.

I remember her asking, "Why don't you act like this at school? The other kids would like you better."

Most kids probably would have been ecstatic to have passed the test, but something inside me snapped. I was hurt and sad. I should have heard that I was fun to hang out with, but I took it as confirmation that she never wanted me there and that the other kids in our class didn't like me.

I became incredibly snippy and mean for the remaining time in her home. When my father picked me up, she hated me again.

My behavior at school was out of control. The teasing from the kids had reached a level where they were not afraid of saying things in front of the teachers, and the teachers didn't stop them. I felt trapped. All day, I had to hang out with kids that saw me as a joke and teachers who wrote me off. Then I would go home and have other struggles to work through.

I started having unusual, unexplainable outbursts.

For whatever reason, I was acting out in gym class. My classmates huddled around the teacher, who was in the process of explaining that day's activities. I was getting impatient and frustrated about the thoughts I couldn't shake from my mind. Suddenly, as if trying to run away from myself, I began running around the gym on all fours like I was a dog. To make matters more embarrassing, I was barking like a dog too. No one was impressed with my abilities, and the teacher was upset I could not get control of myself.

After the incident, the teacher called my father and told him what I had done in class.

As if I had not humiliated myself enough that day, my father had concocted a punishment he seemed too excited to set in motion.

When I got home, he was the only one there. He made me slowly take off my shorts and undies. The sides of my undies scraped along my thighs as I moved them down my legs.

I thought he would make me get on the bed on all fours while he whipped me with the belt. The belt was a typical punishment for me, and it happened often. He would have me take off my clothes and crawl on the bed. My head would push into the pillow as I kept my bottom high in the air. He would strike down with a leather belt, sometimes getting my butt, sometimes my back leaving black and blue marks behind.

This time, he ordered me to keep my shirt on and pull the bottom of the back of my shirt over my head, covering my eyes. I didn't understand at first, so he excitedly showed me what he was asking of me. He grabbed my shirt, pulled my hair to bend my head back, and used my shirt to hold my head.

My father instructed me to "get down on all fours and bark like a dog." I understood at that point what he wanted me to do. My shirt covered my eyes, so I could not see the hits coming. He began to strike my bare bottom with a solid piece of wood. It hurt differently than the belt. I could hear his laughter echoing off the hall walls while the board smacked against my swelling flesh.

He sounded like a person thoroughly enjoying a ride at the fair, getting louder as he hit me when my bark wasn't loud enough or if I stopped moving around the room on all fours. The carpet burned beneath my palms and my knees. My tears dampened my shirt, which clung to my cheeks and pulled my head back as it stretched the fabric. My sobs caught in my throat because the pulling from my shirt was cutting off my ability to breathe.

He continued hitting me until my stepmother came home. He called back to her in excitement. "Come look at this!" he said. I could hear her coming down the hallway. She began hesitantly asking questions, his excitement deflating as he justified and defended his actions. Her lack of enthusiasm must have bored him because it seemed he was no longer having as much fun. He grabbed my shirt and tossed me into my room.

I HAD MADE FRIENDS in the new trailer court. After that punishment, (when I was allowed to leave the house again) I went to a friend's house and told her mother what had happened. I had begun to trust her mother. I also told her I was not doing well in school and my grades were coming home soon. I was afraid because my parents warned me that I would "get it" if I had one fail on my report card.

When I finished telling her what was going on in our home, she called social services and then my stepmother. She told my stepmother I could stay with them. Instead of my stepmother supporting the suggestion, she was furious. She came to the house and started yelling at my friend's mother and me.

"We got your report card today. The lowest grade you got was a D, so you did all this for nothing," she said. Then she directed her attention back to my friend's mother, telling her to mind her business. I was no longer allowed to be friends with that girl.

Like a mighty giant, I roared, but by the time the social worker came to my house, all I had left in me was a whimper.

A stranger sat with me on the deck to ask me questions. I was hesitant to speak. We sat right outside the door next to the living room window. I knew my father was on the other side of the open window listening to every word. I also knew I was already in big trouble because Social Services was sitting on our deck. I had spilled our family secret once again, hoping this time it would stick.

I started trying to explain the situation to the social worker quietly. I whispered to him my father hit me with a two-by-four; this is what my father called it. The social worker immediately started bombarding me with questions.

"Do you know what a two-by-four is? You would be in a lot of pain if he hit you with that. You would probably need a doctor. Why don't you describe to me what a two-by-four is so I know you know what you are saying."

I was immediately scared. I knew this guy would not help me, and I would be in trouble the second he left. I skated around the remaining questions and did a whole lot of squirming. I still hoped the worker would read my mind and get me out of there.

He continued, "Your family loves you. They want you to behave ..." as if he's known us for years and could speak on behalf of these well-rounded adults who had me in their care.

When the social worker finished questioning us, he spoke to my father on the deck. I was on the other side of the living room window this time. I could hear him talking to my father. "You see," my father said, "this is what we have to put up with. She lies all the time and doesn't appreciate all we do for her."

The social worker responded, "If you have any more problems with her, let us know, and we will come out and take care of it."

My heart dropped in my chest as hopelessness flooded my body. I failed myself again. All I had to do was tell the truth and stick to my guns. But now, even Social Services thought I was just a bad kid. *If you have more problems with her? We will take care of it?* What did that even mean? *What will they do to me?* I wondered. I didn't have much time to wonder. Shortly after the man left, my father came into my room and expressed his dislike for my recent transgressions.

Chapter 14

_____

"I cry even harder, thinking of how it could have been, of how I thought it would be. For the first time, I want to give up and die because suddenly everything is too much, and there is no solution in sight."

—B.A. PARIS

M y stepmother's family lived in Arizona. They had met me but did not get to Wisconsin often. We drove down to visit them a couple of times. They were friendly, but I was not as close to them as my grandparents on my father's side.

Things were different in Arizona. Instead of grass, everyone had rocks in their front yard. My grandparents' backyard was a peaceful, fenced-in haven with lush green grass and grapefruit trees. The Arizona heat was both suffocating and wonderful at the same time. I would spend most of my time wandering, trying to make friends. I would play Asteroids on their old computer on the hottest days.

We went out for dinner often. One night my grandparents said we had to try this fantastic restaurant in Glendale called

Kiss the Cook.

We arrived before dark. The restaurant was an intimate, one-story building with a small parking lot. We climbed out of the van, and my grandparents teased me.

"It's called Kiss the Cook because you must kiss the cook when you finish your meal to pay for it."

I stopped dead in my tracks next to the van, my stomach filled with lead. My thoughts echoed in my head. Did they know what he was doing? Now they were going to make me kiss another man?

"I don't believe that," I said. I couldn't believe it. I didn't want to consider it.

My stepmother decided to join the fun and chimed in, confirming I would have to kiss the cook. They all looked down at me and laughed at my reaction.

"Why does it have to be me?" I asked. "Why can't you do it?"

"Because you are the only one not married," my stepmother replied.

"I'm a kid. This isn't right! I shouldn't have to kiss old men!" I yelled in panic.

I couldn't take another step. My head started to spin, and I fell against the car, crying. My response was dramatic and deserved an Academy Award, except I was not acting. My legs refused to hold me up.

Under my breath, I said, "Don't make me kiss him too."

I had yet to hate myself so wholeheartedly. I was helpless and was beginning to believe I would be passed around from one older man's lap to another for the rest of my life.

I was drawing attention in the parking lot, and my family was starting to feel embarrassed. My grandparents were beginning to ask questions.

"What is she talking about?" my grandma asked.

I panicked and watched my father.

Disgust and irritation crossed my father's face as he looked back at me. "Nothing. She has no idea what she is talking about," my father replied. "Niki, knock it off. Let's go."

The joke was no longer entertaining to anyone.

I did not walk right away. Like a helpless fawn, I was too afraid to move. There was no trust between us. I wondered if the adults were changing their story so I would go into the restaurant quietly and be trapped like I had been many times with my father.

"You're so gullible. You get a chocolate kiss at the end of the meal. That's why it's called Kiss the Cook," my father said.

Everyone was silent, my grandmother's attention still on me.

Fearing my father's wrath, I followed them into the restaurant.

We enjoyed our dinner, and later that night, the cook did come to our table. I was terrified, but we all got a chocolate kiss and nothing more. We left that night with the dramatic events eventually fading from everyone's minds. At least no one brought it up again.

It is a feeling I will never forget, a devastating feeling that seemed to suffocate me when my parents convinced me they wanted me to kiss another grown man.

I wonder if my stepmother's parents would have figured it out if we had more time together. How my grandmother looked at my father made me feel like pulling the wool over her eyes would be tough.

Chapter 15

"When fear makes your choices for you, no security measures on earth will keep the things you dread from finding you. But if you can avoid avoidance—if you can choose to embrace experiences out of passion, enthusiasm, and a readiness to feel whatever arises—then nothing, nothing in all this dangerous world, can keep you from being safe."

—MARTHA BECK

My stepmother was very pregnant with what would arrive as a beautiful little girl. She was having a tough time with her second pregnancy. She rarely felt well. She would get a craving and start to make food she thought would satisfy her food cravings, but the smell of the food cooking would send her running down the hall to the bathroom.

During the latter part of her pregnancy, I went on a bit of an adventure, resulting in an accident. Behind the trailer, there was a very tall tree perfect for climbing. There was nothing like being up in a tree, seeing all around but not being noticed by others. Climbing trees felt more natural to me than walking on the ground, and I proved it that day.

I could see my brother down below. He was looking for me, so I maneuvered down from my hiding place, stretching my arms and legs to reach the branches as I descended. Safely on the ground, I walked up a small hill toward my brother. In a split second, my face planted into the soil. My arm and head hurt instantly. I groaned and looked over my shoulder, where I could see my shoe had caught a lifted root from my favorite tree.

I tried to push up from my hands, but the pressure on my right wrist was too much. Oh no, I broke my wrist again. Dad is going to kill me. I had broken my left wrist in third grade, but this hurt way more. My brother knew something was wrong, too, as he shifted from his left foot to his right, repeating, "Are you okay?"

"Go get Mom! I need help!"

But my sweet young brother couldn't get help. He could only pace and repeatedly ask if I was okay. His fear overwhelmed him.

I used my legs to get off the ground and my left hand to open our trailer's back door to find my stepmother.

My stepmother was upset immediately.

"You know you are not supposed to climb trees! Why were you up there?"

"I wasn't climbing! I mean, I was, but ..."

"You were climbing!"

"No, yes, but no. That's not how this happened. I was not in the tree anymore! Please, it really hurts. I think I need to go to the hospital."

"I can't drive to the hospital, and your father just fell asleep."

My father was working the late shift and would sleep right when he came home. She did not want to wake him, and I didn't want to either. His anger would be uncontrollable! But my wrist hurt. I couldn't move it, and it swelled up quickly. After a few hours, my stepmother woke him up, and he took me to the hospital.

I was not allowed to get up from my bed in the hospital. I had my first experience with a cold, metal bedpan. I felt like I had peed all over myself, but the nurse assured me I had not. The doctors gave me medicine, and I was put to sleep to fix my wrist.

My wrist had swelled so badly that I needed a temporary cast until the swelling went down.

The pain was too much for me that evening. My arm hurt so much that my stomach hurt, and I believed I was dying of internal bleeding. I have no recollection of what would have made me think this. I was scared, but comfort was not in the cards. My stepmother, exhausted from her pregnancy, and my father spent from a day without sleep, made it so yelling was all I received when I cried out in pain.

The next day, my grandparents came to pick me up. I always felt safe and loved when I was with my grandparents. Our adventures are my best memories.

My aunt worked down the street at the local grocery store. When I was younger, my grandma would pull coins out of the Snoopy bank she had for me, and we'd walk down to get candy and say hello. At night, she would rub my back and tell me stories of funny memories I created just being me.

She shared her favorite memory, and thus my favorite. "You were so cute playing by the church when you saw me sweeping. You walked over because you wanted to help. You were adamant that you wanted to help me. So, I went inside and searched and found a second broom. You gave a few sweeps, stopped, handed me the broom, and said, 'Grandma, I broom later,' then took off to find more frogs."

Then we would laugh together. Before I knew it, I would be asleep.

My grandfather was the strong, silent type. He was full of love but often worked hard at his sermons. When he wasn't working, we would drive around and either get something to eat or go to the mall.

My grandfather bought me my first bra!

He had told my father I needed to be wearing a bra. I was becoming a woman, and there was no hiding my development under my Bart Simpson t-shirt. My father had argued with him in the kitchen and eventually told my grandfather he should buy me a bra if he had a problem with my exposed breasts.

Grandpa walked me into Sears and asked a lady who worked there to help fit me for my first bra. She was older and had curly thick, tinseled hair held back with a barrette. She peered down at me through her thick wide-rimmed glasses.

"I can help her, sure."

"Good, if you need me, I will be *way* over there," he said as he pointed to the opposite side of the store. I had never seen him so embarrassed. That same day he bought me my first bottle of perfume, Elizabeth Arden Sunflowers.

My grandfather and my grandmother were my light. Like angels, they watched over me.

ONE NIGHT, my grandma had driven a long way to babysit my brother and me. My parents had taken my new sister with them on their date. I was supposed to be in bed at a specific time, but if you had a grandma as awesome as mine, you know bedtime doesn't exist in babysitting land. My brother was already asleep. The poor guy couldn't hang. But Grandma and I sat up and talked and laughed.

A flash of light scanned the kitchen window, sounding the alarm that my parents were home. "Hurry up now. Hugs. I love you," my grandmother said as she ushered me into the hall.

It was past my bedtime, so I fell right to sleep, barely hearing the muffled voices in the living room as my parents entered our home. A few hours later, I woke up around one in the morning and immediately felt something was off. I didn't know what I felt, but I knew something was different. The house felt cold, darker than usual.

My brother's room was next to mine, and I could enter it through the shared bathroom. I walked through our bathroom into my brother's bedroom to check on him, but he was not there. I didn't understand what was happening. I started looking for him in his room. I checked his toy box under his bed. Sometimes, he sleepwalked and was found in unusual places.

Finally, I panicked and ran to my parents' bedroom. In the dark, I whispered to my stepmother. I whispered louder and louder, but she never responded. I crept over to their bed and felt for her, but she was not there. I listened but couldn't hear any breathing or snoring. I turned on the lights, prepared to ignite my father's unhappy voice.

In a flash, the room revealed my biggest fear. There was no one in the house. My sister was gone, my parents were gone, and I couldn't find my brother.

I ran through the trailer turning on all the lights. I

was alone.

I was often left alone but always locked in my room. I returned to the kitchen phone and dialed my grandmother's number. She answered the phone in a groggy voice.

"Grandma, are you sure my parents were home before you left?"

"What?" she said, trying to piece together what I was saying.

"Are you sure my parents were home before you left?" I repeated.

"Yes, of course, Niki. What's wrong?"

"There is no one here. I looked in their beds. Everyone is gone, and I don't understand. It's late. Where could they be? Nothing is open."

"It's going to be okay, Niki. Grandpa is on his way."

"What!? No, no, Grandpa can't come. I'll get in trouble."

I felt intense fear. If my father came back to find his father here, I would be in big trouble, like Social Services trouble.

"Niki, you can't be there alone. Grandpa is on his way," my grandma replied.

My grandfather drove to our home, a forty-five-minute drive. He arrived just seconds before my family arrived, just before two in the morning. My mother's face was twisted in shock as she walked up the steps to find my grandfather, who walked straight to my father outside.

My father and grandfather fought loudly, their relationship unraveling before me. Grandpa yelled something I can barely recall, something about my father destroying me. My father shouted back. I remember feeling shocked and thankful my grandfather firmly stuck up for me. But then my grandfather left, and my hope went with him.

My parents were out with friends that night. They had come home to relieve my grandmother from her babysitting duties. After my grandmother left, they took my brother and sister to meet with their friends for coffee. They told me this as if to justify their actions and made me feel bad about everything that transpired from my phone call to my grandma, saying things like "You're obviously not mature enough to be left at home," and "You're the reason we won't be visiting Grandma and Grandpa."

A few years passed before I was allowed to be with my grandparents again. That fight temporarily severed the relationship between my father and grandfather. In my early teen years, my grandparents sat me down and suggested I come live with them. I do not know if they had figured out exactly what was happening at home, but they must have caught on. They told me I could live with them, but I would need to start over. I would have to go to a new school. The decision was up to me.

A part of me screamed in delight at the idea of being in a home where I was always safe. Another part of me was scared. A new school, again. I thought of my brother and my new little sister alone with my father. What would he do to them? My father said I would never see them if I moved in with my grandparents. Somehow, I believed I could protect them from him.

Fear led me to a decision I would forever regret. I said no.

Sometimes, staying in a place of fear is easier than being free. This is because a place of fear feels familiar, and for some reason, that makes us feel safer than the unknown.

Chapter 16

"Anger is the acid that can do more harm to the vessel in which it is stored than to anything on which it is provided."

—MARK TWAIN

nger has a distinct way of sculpting a person's facial features. Even without a word, another will immediately recognize the emotion for what it is. As I grew, I seemed to have developed a unique ability to make my father angry, and when I did, there were generally three types of punishments I could expect.

One form of punishment would involve chores. My father would have me cut the weeds growing alongside the trailer with a pair of scissors. I would bundle them up and discard them in the ditch behind the house. I learned to mow the grass with a manual mower. We had a good old-fashioned manual push walk-behind reel lawnmower, which didn't work well because I was not tall enough. We also had a gas mower I was not allowed to use.

Mowing was not a chore I was required to do often. The outdoor whining attracted too much attention from the neighbors, who felt I was too young and too short to be using the equipment provided. My father did not appreciate their concern.

My father built a wooden sandbox for my brother and his friends. It reminded me of a picnic table. It was designed for kids to sit on the box's sides as if they were at a picnic table, and the tabletop was a box filled with sand. I was not allowed to play in it, even if my brother wanted to play with me.

"I did not build it for you. Stay away from him," my father said more than once.

I did get to paint it, though.

Chores like these were not my enemy. I enjoyed having something to do, and there were rare occasions when I would finish working on something, and it felt good. In scarce instances, my work was to my father's satisfaction. Occasional moments of feeling like I was enough were what kept me going.

The second form of common punishment was being locked in my room or having things in my room taken away. My father had nailed my bedroom window shut a while back—preemptive strike, maybe?

One evening, I was excited to go to Chuck E. Cheese. I had heard my parents talking about it, but the invitation did not include me. My parents packed up my new sister and almost three-year-old brother and locked me in my room.

There were many celebrations my family would exclude me from, and my heart never accepted it. Each time I sat crying on the floor or watched out the window as they left, a part of my hoping that they would return to get me.

MY FAMILY DID NOT tolerate my imagination. For example, I learned the art of creating floor dens from a kids TV show. I put my blankets and pillow on my bedroom floor to build a fort. When my father saw this, he was outraged.

"You are a spoiled brat. That bed is not good enough for you? You don't appreciate anything! You deserve nothing!" he yelled as he ripped my blankets from underneath me and grabbed my pillow.

"You don't like your bed? Then you don't get to sleep in it! Maybe this will make you appreciate what you have!" He took my blankets and pillows from me and made me sleep on the floor.

When my father realized I was using my clothes to keep warm at night, he took those away, too, until there was nothing I could find to keep me warm.

ONE DAY, I missed the bus from school. I called my dad to ask him to pick me up. He told me to start walking, and if the teacher asked, I was to inform them he would pick me up down the road. He did not pick me up. I now know it was a three-and-a-half-mile walk.

I enjoyed my long walk home so much that I began to miss the bus on purpose. I'd even swing into a local bakery to get a free donut hole. When my father discovered I was enjoying myself, he made sure I wouldn't ever want to miss the bus again by using the third form of discipline—his favorite—the one he used most often.

His voice would pierce through the air like an arrow straight through my gut. *Here it comes*, I would think to myself. His red face twisted, and his eyes grew too wide for their sockets. My head would drop down automatically, avoiding all eye contact. If I looked him in the eyes, it would enrage him more. His hand would grab my arm and pull me into his room like a three-year-old girl carelessly holding her doll.

Immediately, tears would flood my eyes because I knew what would happen. I often did not understand why I was in trouble. My father tossed me onto his bed and pulled at my pants, trying to release them from my hips to my ankles. My hands would grab at my pants, trying to keep them pulled up, but it was a fight I had never won.

With a quick flip, I would be on my belly with his hands on my hips as he pulled me into position. My arms grasped at the ruffled blankets on the bed. Tears of fear and confusion wet the pillow he stuffed my head into. I struggled to breathe while I twisted my head for more air. But I had learned not to lift my head or turn around.

Once, I flipped around mid-discipline to see the belt high above his head, ready to strike. It came down with full force toward my head. My forearm reached up just in time to protect my face from the blow of the belt.

He smiled.

"See? Should have kept your ass in the air. Now get it up."

He would laugh while he hit me. Black and blue welts raised on my bare bottom, but they wouldn't stop him. He would strike down on me while yelling,

"Do you like that? Get your ass up. I said get it up!"

For years, I would cry from the blinding pain. I hated it all. I hated myself, I hated him, I hated my life, I hated God. When he wasn't getting off on my chest, he would cause mind-numbing pain that temporarily seemed to satisfy his other urges. After some years, I quit crying and laid on the bed lifeless, nothing but a young girl's hollow shell.

IT WAS TIME to move again. People often ask how I remember my age through the many incidences I share. Because there was no consistency, we moved often, and I changed schools often. This makes it easy for me to separate where I was and what I was going through at the time.

We moved out of the trailer into a house closer to school. For a short time, so much work was needed in the home that my father didn't have time to discipline me. Once we were settled in, life as I knew it was back to *normal*.

In sixth grade, I had another outburst in school that exposed my truth. I was tired of being picked on. One of the basketball players asked why I was such a loser, and in a fast-paced vent session, I told the whole room what was happening at home and how long it had been going on.

When I finished, I realized I was standing at my desk, crying and breathless, and everyone's eyes were on me.

I was pulled out of class and placed near a teacher's lounge window. I sat for hours waiting for the teacher to return. My teacher came in with the principal (her husband) and sat down to talk to me.

"We called your father," she said. My heart dropped into my stomach. I felt betrayed, isolated, and once again filled with fear because I knew what would happen when I got home.

"He says you've done this before, that you tell people this lie when things don't go well for you. He said Social Services had come out and found nothing. If your words were true, they would have found something," she said.

"So, I am lying," I said flatly. My eyes swelled up, but I would not let a tear fall. Anger seeped into the deepest part of my being. No matter who I shared my story with, no one would believe me, and because I spoke up again, there would be hell to pay when I got home.

"There are far too many silent sufferers. Not because they don't yearn to reach out, but because they've tried and found no one who cares."

—RICHELLE E. GOODRICH

Chapter 17

"The only real prison is fear, and the only real freedom is freedom from fear."

—AUNG SAN SUU KYI

At twelve years old, endless calls from the school with extensive reports of how I misbehaved were the norm. I started smoking, drinking, and staying away from home as much as possible. I would leave without permission and take the heat when I came back. It was better than being alone with him.

I had one friend—my best friend. We would go on adventures together. At first, they were innocent, but over time, they turned into drinking, smoking, and hanging out with older men—not the kind of men I would want with my daughter.

My father invited my best friend over repeatedly, but I was not too fond of how he looked at her, and she said he made her uncomfortable, not that I could blame her. We spent most of our time at her house watching movies like *Scream*. It was Skeet Ulrich for her, Matthew Lillard for me. We went to *Titanic* a couple of hundred times and *Romeo and Juliet* because Leonardo DiCaprio was all the rage.

I often overstayed my welcome at my friend's house because I would have done anything never to have to go home again. Fear kept me from telling her what had been happening at home. I thought she would look at me differently, and the last two times I told my best friend, I was never allowed to see them again. I even had to switch schools.

My smothering proved too much for our friendship. Eventually, I overstayed my welcome, and our friendship was over.

I WAS BEGINNING to get sassy on a whole new level. I learned the more difficult I was, the more physical abuse I endured, but the sexual abuse was less.

When he'd hit me, throw me into the wall, grab my hair and pull me down the stairs by it, I felt nothing physically. Emotionally, I was angry instead of scared. Adrenaline fueled my rage and made me feel powerful. It was like he wanted to kill me but couldn't because I simply wouldn't die. I felt unbreakable. That felt better than the hollow feeling inside when he touched me.

As long as I kept him angry at me, my body was safe from his sexual touch. I would endure anything if it meant I wouldn't have to feel the sickness eating my soul. When he touched me, I imagined I was being buried alive. The dark place I would go in my mind felt suffocating. I could feel the burning sensation in my lungs from the dirt entering as I inhaled. My skin tingled from the legs of tiny bugs crawling and the ground shifting around me. My ears would strain to hear any sign of someone coming to save me, but no one ever did.

During one of our usual altercations, in which he dragged me down the stairs by my hair, my father shared news meant to terrify me. Instead, it sparked a relief I hadn't felt in a long time.

"You ungrateful bitch. You have no idea how good you have it. You think you have it bad here? Just wait until you meet your mother."

My head snapped up. He said what?! My mind filled quickly with questions and hope. The hateful words he continued to spill from his snake-like tongue were now blocked by my voice screaming in my head. *My mother? The woman I was never allowed to see again? The woman who was NOT my mother? The one you would lie to and tell I wasn't home to talk? That mother? Are my sisters with her? Will we all live together? I will never come back here!!*My father had tracked down my mother because he thought she could help me see how lucky I was to live with him. Not that she was in on any plan, he just assumed I would want to come home if I met her—at least that's what he said.

I wasn't allowed to stay with my mother, though. I had to stay with my mema and papa, and he was all too happy to warn me I would be returning "home."

My father sent me on a plane to Texas when the day came. My first plane experience. I was unsure whether I was more scared or excited; both feelings seemed to echo each other inside me.

We walked up to the gate. Once my father made sure I was in the right area, he set to leave. There was no care or concern in his voice, only impatience and irritation. He was still upset about the additional plane ride cost for a lone child to fly.

People packed themselves into the plane as the flight attendant introduced herself to me. She said she would be keeping an eye on me, and I would be safe.

Lady, you have no idea, I thought to myself. I smiled.

I had an aisle seat. Like any kid, I wanted to look outside, so I twisted my neck and leaned as far as possible. Most of my experience has blurred over time, but I remember my ears hurting something fierce when we went up in the air. The lady beside me gave me a piece of gum, and the flight attendant provided some lemon-lime fizzy drink. Together, they seemed to release the pain.

When I arrived, giant hugs, squeals, and laughter from my sister, aunt, and papa welcomed me. My other sister lived with someone else, not near where I would be staying. I had never met my aunt or my papa. They looked down at me like I was the missing piece of their hearts. I felt at home before we even left the airport.

Texas was different from Wisconsin. It was flat and dry, and the air felt different. It wrapped around me like a warm blanket, fresh from the dryer, causing me to sweat and stay dry simultaneously.

My mother was not at the airport to greet me. She lived in the city and occasionally stopped by Mema and Papa's house, but we didn't share much time. I did stay the night at her apartment a few times until I got bedbugs, and Mema didn't want me staying there anymore.

I shared a room with my sister at Mema and Papa's country ranch-style home. They had a lot of land to explore and a few cows to booty slap and hall ass away. Papa was my mother's father, and Mema was his second wife. We had never met prior. She was a no-bullshit kind of gal. Mema had no problem calling anyone out and cutting through their excuses. As a teenager, it was a bit much. As an adult, she is one of my heroes.

One aunt lived close by with her husband, daughter, and son, and another aunt lived in the same city as my mother. I had never met this side of my family before either, yet I felt like I belonged.

My sister and I occasionally fought because I wouldn't let her breathe. I had never looked up to anyone like I had her. I wanted to be her. She was funny, strong, and also a no-bullshit southern girl. Her CD player had Mariah Carey on repeat. We played Frogger regularly and camped in the backyard when we weren't looking for trouble.

Surrounded by a new family, you'd think I would have shined like a new penny. However, my change in location did not remove my pain. I was still angry, defensive, cautious, and needy. My family did not know why I was this way. They didn't understand my outbursts and bitter attitude. Truthfully, I didn't understand either. Each episode would leave me confused, embarrassed, and unworthy of love.

One night my aunt picked up some things from the store for me. I was unhappy with what she picked up because it was not exactly what I requested, so I caught an attitude. She pulled me aside and set me straight.

"Look, I don't know what happened to you up there, and it's clear something did, but you are not there anymore. We love you, but your attitude is awful. Here I am doing you a favor, and you are taking advantage of me, being rude, and acting spoiled."

Did she say WE LOVE you? I looked up at her and blinked back my tears.

There was a long pause between us.

She wasn't manipulating me. She didn't purposely try to

make me feel like the worst person in the world. She spoke to me like I was an adult. I suddenly felt older than I was.

"I am sorry. I am very grateful for you, and I love you too. I will try to do better," I said while trying to catch my tears. When my aunt hugged me, my floodgates opened.

While I paint the *Pleasantville* version of my summer, I should probably tell you my family was not perfect. Whose is? Many in my family fought alcohol and drug addiction. Many struggled to keep their apartments and jobs. Every night was a party, but this life was acceptable to me as a young teen. It was all I ever wanted to do, anyway.

One thing they didn't do was put their crap on me. I never felt unsafe. The family I was surrounded by didn't manipulate or use me. There was no violence toward me. They had their demons too, but they loved me and made sure I knew it.

My summer was the best one I had ever had. There were late-night fires, band practice, hot summer walks, days at the pool, family, video games, and more. I learned a lot about myself. But it had to end.

I had to go back to Wisconsin. There were some I missed at home, like my brother and sister, but there was no part of me that wanted to return "home." In Texas, I was not someone's property—I was a person with feelings and a personality. Before I left, I swore I would return to Texas, even if I had to walk back.

Chapter 18

"Success is the sum of small efforts,
repeated day in and day out."

—ROBERT COLLIER

Back in Wisconsin, our family dynamic had changed again.

The perfect home image we projected was under attack and losing face quickly. My father and stepmother had been fighting for months. I remember vividly some of the things he said because I felt them. I felt for her.

At first, it was nice the attention was off me. But then a strange woman started sleeping in my brother's bed, and things became very tense in the home.

My father and stepmother's separation progressed, and the marriage was over. Nothing about it was good. There are many memories I could share, but their relationship is not my story to tell.

I had been a significant brat to my stepmother, but not because I didn't love her. I had been screaming for help through my actions throughout her relationship with my father. I didn't realize she had been crying for help as well.

On the final night of their in-house fighting, I crouched by the railing and listened to the harsh words they spat at each other. Then he spoke the last sentence he used to cut her deep. That sentence rings in my head to this day and makes me feel insecure as a woman. So much so that I won't ever repeat it out loud.

Her only crime, as far as I was concerned, was that she loved him. Nothing she did was ever enough, and she was never right. I realized that day I was not alone in my abuse. I saw my stepmother in a new light.

After he stormed out, I snuck downstairs and allowed myself to tell her I was sorry for always being trouble for her. I cried and told her I loved her, and I did. And I know she loved me too.

VERY LITTLE TIME PASSED until a new family moved in. I liked the woman he was seeing. She was smart, strong, and sassy. She also had two daughters. However, this switch into an instant family did not change his desires toward me as I thought it would.

It was early afternoon, and my soon-to-be second stepmother was not home yet. I had just stepped out of the upstairs shower. The bathroom separated my bedroom from my parent's, with my brother's bedroom across the hall. We could see through the railing into the living room downstairs from the bathroom.

I scanned my teenage body in the mirror, hating everything I saw. I had grown stocky. My thick thighs rested right below my pudgy, bloated belly. My breasts were round, too large for a girl of my height and body. It was as though a stranger was looking back at me.

I rotated my backside to expose it in the mirror and noticed an unusual mole in the center of my back. It was a bit large, and I didn't remember seeing it before. I reached back to touch the dark spot that rested just above my buttocks but couldn't quite get to it.

Upon closer inspection, I realized the mole had legs. I shrieked. It was not a mole. It was a tick! I didn't remember ever having a tick on me before. I had heard I could die if the head stayed in when pulling them out.

I grabbed a towel to wrap around myself and panicked. I didn't know what to do. I didn't want to show my father's girlfriend my backside, and I didn't want to show my father, who was the only one at home. He had not made advances toward me since my trip to Texas. Still, I didn't want to be in the same room as him. I felt helpless as I desperately tried to reach the tick.

I gave up.

I yelled, "Dad, I have a tick on my back. How do I get it out?"

"A tick? Let's see."

I pulled the towel back just a bit.

He looked in on my backside while I watched him from the mirror.

"You do. I will get it. Come with me."

"It's okay. I can get it out if you just tell me what to do."

He looked back at me, irritated. "Do you want my help or not."

I sucked in my breath. "Okay, let me get dressed quick," I said and started walking to my room.

"No, I don't have time. Get in here," he replied.

I paused from the way he said it. A familiar feeling crept into my stomach, dropping like a ton of bricks wrapped in barbed wire that twisted and rolled around my insides.

I stopped in the hall, bare feet on the smooth wood floor, my body wrapped tightly by my towel. My head looked straight ahead at my bedroom door, my inner monologue streaming. *How could I be so stupid? Why didn't I wait for her to come home? I could tell him to forget it and deal with it myself. But how am I going to deal with something I can't reach? I can wait for her to get home. It would be far better to ask her. What was I thinking? FUCK.* "Hurry up. You don't need clothes on." His voice pulled me out of my thoughts.

My eyes shut as I swallowed the lump of bile back down my throat and slowly turned around to walk toward his room. *I can do this. As soon as he pulls this gross thing out of me, I will hightail it back to my room.* When I spun around and peered into his room, I saw he was undressed.

"Just going to take a shower quickly, but I'll help you with the tick first. Come bend over the bed so I can see it better," he said.

I wrapped the towel tighter, lowered my head, and moved slowly toward the bed. As I passed him, he ripped the towel from my skin, exposing my body.

"You won't need this." He smiled as he pointed his finger and circled it around, instructing me to turn toward the bed. I could feel him slide up behind me. His leg brushed against mine, his penis resting on my buttocks while his fingers poked at the tick in the center of my back. My face was stuck in the pillow like it had been so many times before. My arms and legs felt weak.

No, no, this is not happening again. What if I kicked him? He would kick my ass. So what? It would be worth it. What if I yelled? If no one heard me—again—butt kicked, or at the very least, mouth slapped.

I started to grow impatient as I panicked.

"Just get it out. Just get it out."

He grabbed the nasty little bug and pulled it out.

"There it is," he said with a big smile, satisfied with his work.

I quickly whipped my body around, grabbed my towel, and attempted to sprint toward my room. My father halted my escape as he stood in front of the door and instructed me to wait. He disposed of the tick in the bathroom and came back muttering under his breath. His energy had changed. He was irritated.

My eyes stretched wide with fear. Standing near the bed with my tight towel, I stepped back. *Here it comes.*

My distress lowered a little as I registered he was getting dressed. *Shit, what did I do to piss him off? What is happening right now? What do I do?*

"Go get your clothes on," he said in a harsh whisper through tight lips.

He sped past me, down the stairs, just in time for me to hear a woman's voice say, "What's going on up there?"

His girlfriend had come home early.

My body released all tension as I let out a thankful breath. I peered down the stairs through the railing and locked eyes with hers. My feet propelled me from their room to mine. My father followed her gaze, which was closed in on me.

"What? Oh, stop. I was removing a tick. What do you think was going on?" he replied in his defense and walked away from her. I stood on the other side of my wall, listening. She stood in place for a few minutes before walking away.

Something in my gut told me she didn't believe him.

Chapter 19

"You may have to fight a battle more than once to win it."

—MARGARET THATCHER

Our bathroom was my Pandora's box of nightmares, specifically the shower. I would get in trouble if I snuck in ours in the morning or took a shower for more than five minutes.

As I grew, I noticed I didn't look like other girls. All of the girls in my class were athletic or thin. My body changed from a slim figure to the body of an emotional eater.

I was a young teenager. My father had started coming into the bathroom a few years prior when no one else was home. At first, it was to brush his teeth or get something from the medicine cabinet. Then he needed to use the restroom, even though there was one upstairs.

As time passed, he found reasons to get closer and closer to the shower curtain. One day, while on the toilet, he asked if I needed someone to scrub my back as if there usually were a person to perform this duty, and they were taking a sick day.

Panic caused me to shiver under the hot water. The voice I

had wanted to run from since I was a young girl was outside my shower curtain now. Before these incidences began, the shower was the one place I felt I could get away and wash clean of his stain.

I stood in our cream-colored, small squared shower. I declined his suggestion, but "you need your back scrubbed" became more of a statement than a question.

A button on our shower head would conserve the water when pushed in. He threw back the curtain and pushed the button to stop the water flow. "Turn around," he said.

"I'm fine. I don't need any help."

"Turn around."

I turned around slowly and looked down at my chubby belly, plump thighs, and awkward knees. I could feel my father's callous hands moving the soap suds around my back.

After a few minutes, he said, "There ya go." I spun back around quickly. My hands covered my breasts, squeezing them together as I stood as far back into the shower as I could. He reached up to the button and pressed it, causing a rush of warm water to hit my side. His hands lifted to the head of the shower to rinse the soap between his fingers. When he finished, he shut the curtain and walked away.

I started to sigh in relief. My muscles tensed again when my father's voice interrupted the silence. "Hurry up. You're all clean now. No need to waste water," he said.

I waited until I heard the bathroom door close before stepping out of the shower.

I don't know what made me think that incident would be a one-time thing. Whenever he asked if I wanted him to wash my back, I said no. Not once did *no* stop him.

The next time he came in while I was showering, he pulled back the curtain and told me to turn around. This time he scrubbed my back, my butt, and down my legs. My body wiggled away as I told him I could reach there and didn't need his help, but he didn't stop.

When the curtain closed, I stood in the shower with my arms wrapped around my chest, hugging my shoulders tightly. I was never going to get away.

To limit his ability to reach me while in the shower, I started to sneak a shower in the morning. I was not allowed to take a shower in the morning because that time was for other family members—anyone other than me.

When my father discovered I was taking showers in the morning, I was in trouble. I'd argue that it wasn't fair. I was the only one with the rule. I even tried to drop loud hints as to why I was only allowed a shower at a specific time of day, but nothing changed.

THE FIRST DRAFT OF MY BOOK did not contain the next written piece. I was not ready to face what was done to me when I was thirteen years old, to expose the vulnerable, intimate situations my father put me in that caused unsurmountable shame and guilt. It was one of the last memories I dared to share with my therapist. As I write this, the same pain, shame, embarrassment, and hatred I felt, again and again, causes a deep sadness in my heart.

After many intrusions of him coming into the bathroom while I was there, each time cleaning more and more of my body, he progressed to the point that almost broke me.

I stood in the shower, cold. My body rinsed, and the water shut off temporarily so he could ensure I was "soaped from head to toe" and everything in between. I felt disgusting while his callused hands explored my young skin.

I'd feel his rough hands scrubbing up my legs. He'd tell me to squat as he put soap on his finger and shoved it inside me, wiggling it in circles. He no longer wore clothes while he cleaned my body. I stared past him while awkwardly squatting, feeling numb, sick, and hollow.

Then one day, he did not come into the shower.

I was finished rinsing on this particular day, thankful he had not come into the bathroom. A safe peace washed over me as I opened the shower curtain and stepped out of the shower.

He was standing, naked, staring at himself in the medicine cabinet mirror.

"Come here," he said. "I can't find the tweezers. Check for me." I grabbed my towel and wrapped it around my frame.

"I don't know where they are," I said while looking for my clothes, which were not where I had left them. I had started bringing clothes to the bathroom since the incident with the tick, but they were gone.

I wrapped my towel tighter around my body and walked past the mirror to leave the bathroom.

"You don't need this," he said as he snatched my towel from my skin in one swift motion. In doing so, he pulled me back into the bathroom corner.

As I stood, staring at him with my back against the wall, my arms covering my breasts, I said, "No. Please give me my towel."

"Check. Top shelf."

Feeling trapped and cautious, I stood on my tippy toes to look, one hand still covering my breasts. Suddenly, his hips pushed into mine, and he was behind me. I could feel his naked waist against my butt.

He began kissing me and probing me as I squirmed. My

wet skin slid between him and the sink. The hard edge of the counter dug into my hips as he pushed me into it. I started to wiggle away, but he tackled me to the ground and was on top of me in seconds. His hands were poking at my ribs, pinning me to the ground. I could feel his penis between my legs as he began to kiss my lips, his meaty hands tangled in my hair. The cold tile pressed against my back. The weight of him pushed the air out of my lungs.

I panicked while he continued to moan on top of me. I knew I had to get out of there fast, but he was too heavy and picking up steam. I did the only thing I thought could work, even though I didn't have much faith in stopping him. I pretended to hear someone come home.

"I heard the door open!" I exclaimed. He stopped and listened. "Didn't you hear that!" I said in a panic. "She's home!"

His eyes were wide, and his ears pulled back as he strained to listen, but he did not get off me.

I tried to move from under him again, but he had me pinned.

"There! You hear that!?" I said, though there was nothing to hear.

He released me. "Hurry upstairs and get dressed."

As I ran out of the bathroom, I saw my clothes on the kitchen table.

I wish she would come home. Catch you, scream at you, and finally expose you for what you are. No talking your way out of that one! How are you going to explain away or justify this shit?! You couldn't. I would be free, she would be free, and you could just go to hell.

Anger swelled inside me, but the truth was I was scared. There was nothing I would be able to do to stop him.

My quick thinking helped me get away that day, but I knew if I didn't do something quick, he would get what he had been after.

I CONTINUED TO TRY to shower when there were others in the house. The family dynamic was still transitioning at times. His girlfriend had two children too. So, there were four kids in the house and her at times. But on this day, my sister and brother were with their mother, and her two children were out. Still, she was home, so I wandered into the bathroom for a shower. I was unaware she was stepping out to get cigarettes.

I was getting out of the shower when my father called me to his room, stating he wanted to show me something. I wasn't concerned because I thought she was home. I had brought my clothes into the bathroom (and kept them close), so I dressed before entering his room.

"What's up?"

"Come look in this drawer."

I walked over to their dresser.

"See these?"

"Yeah."

"They're vibrators."

"Gross." I turned to walk away.

"Are you calling [girlfriend] gross?"

"No. I'm just ..."

"Get on the bed."

He pulled out a little tan one. "Pull down your pants."

"I do not want to use that."

"You need to learn about your body." His voice went from sweet to aggressive. "I am just going to take a look."

"I don't need you to take a look."

His facial muscles tightened.

"Where's [girlfriend]?"

"She's getting cigarettes. Lay on the bed."

I knew I had two choices: run and get dragged back to the room by my hair (it wouldn't have been the first time) or get on the bed and hope it would be over quickly.

I could see his head between my legs. He smiled as he examined my body. He acted as if he were doing me an excellent service, showing me "where I would instruct a man to touch me to please me." I squirmed away from his fingers, pressing on my fresh fourteen-year-old innocence.

"That hurts. I don't think that's right. I don't like it. Stop doing that," I said, my voice getting louder and angrier.

I continued to wiggle away. He'd grab my legs and pull me back.

His smile turned to a frown as he began looking at my lady parts like an intricate puzzle. "No, this is right. It should make you feel good," he said, frustrated.

"Well, it doesn't," I said, irritated. "It hurts. Maybe I'm not normal. Maybe there is something wrong with me. Maybe I need to see a doctor. Maybe [girlfriend] could help me understand my body," I said indifferently.

Shock stretched his face in a way I had never seen before.

My spark was gone. I didn't care what happened to me anymore. Beat me, rape me, stab me. I didn't care. There was no use fighting. No one was coming to save me, and nothing I had ever done stopped this monster.

He stood up and stared down at me. I had never seen on him whatever his emotion was that day. "Well, they are in her top drawer if you want them," he said and walked out of the room to finish mowing the lawn, leaving the tan vibrator on the bed.

A spark ignited deep inside me. I had figured it out. My father liked the crying, and he wanted the fight. My mocking and disinterest did not please him. *I did it. I control him now. He won't want to touch me again.* A bold statement, but I thought I had it all figured out.

As I walked to my room with a strut, I heard my soon-to-be stepmother's voice downstairs asking him what was wrong. He said nothing, but she wouldn't let up. He walked outside and slammed the door.

Shortly after, she called my name from the bottom of the stairs. I walked to my bedroom door and peered down. "What is your dad's problem?" she asked.

"I don't know," I replied.

"What did you do!" she yelled.

"I didn't do anything!" My voice rose with hers. *How could she be yelling at me?*

This accusation was the last straw for me. I was tired of being this bully's plaything while his wives were away. My sassy attitude thickened. Come hell or high water. I was going to get out of this house. Already a delinquent, I became uncontrollable, a *heathen*, a *martyr*, and a *bitch*.

Chapter 20

"One should rather die than be betrayed. There is no deceit in death. It delivers precisely what it has promised. Betrayal, though ... betrayal is the willful slaughter of hope."

—STEVEN DIETZ

High school began, and it did not take me long to connect with other troubled youth. We had a distinct attitude about us, one that clearly stated we didn't give a shit. The older delinquents would show newbies the way of our people—where to hide between class, get smokes and alcohol, that sort of thing.

It was customary for "difficult" teens to skip class. Since I quit caring about myself, I had no intention of caring about school. Some kids would go back home when their parents had gone to work, while others would hang out by the shops nearby or hide under a viaduct by the school. Either way, you could find us smoking, drinking, and laughing away our cares as the school time clock counted down our inevitable walk back to our prisons, mental or otherwise.

I preferred the viaducts. It was an easy walk alongside a

fence behind the school. I'd hop the fence, cross the train tracks, and wait for class to be over. The spray-painted graffiti covering the underside of the viaduct kept my companions and me entertained. I can still remember some of the "poems."

Sex, drugs, rock and roll
Weed, speed, birth control
Life's a bitch, and then you die
Fuck the world; let's all get high.
Or
LSD in my tea
Gummy bears are chasing me
Some are green; some are blue
The yellow one just stole my shoe.

Creativity at its best. We would gather underneath with our Tropicana drinks and Combos snacks and dream of a life without our parents. One day our fantasy of being free got out of control.

The last day I spent under the viaduct was with three other young teenage kids sick of dealing with their life—abusive parents, foster parents, and missing parents. We all told our stories about our situations at home. I shared minor details about my father's physical abuse to explain my Texas experience and how much I missed it. History taught me not to share too much.

"Let's run away right now," my boyfriend of a week said. We had no food or water, no extra clothing, and no money.

"We can't," I said. "How are we going to get to Texas without any money?"

The other two girls were on board, chiming in with excitement. I was hesitant as I listened to him excitedly share about his uncle, who lived a few towns away, and stated he would take us if we could get to him.

"Okay, let me just call my dad and tell him I am running away," I replied after much convincing.

"What! No!" my friends exclaimed in unison.

"No, don't worry. He doesn't care about me at all. He isn't going to care if I run away. He'll finally be happy, I bet," I replied. (At this time, I did not understand gaslighting and the need for control in abuse.)

They did convince me not to call my father. We grabbed our backpacks and started walking.

We walked the bluffs the rest of the day and into the evening, staying away from the roads. I was so thirsty at one point that I snuck into someone's yard and drank from the hose.

That night the stars were bright. We were tired, and we decided to rest. We lay down in a cornfield and started to fall asleep. I don't remember what spooked us, but something prompted us to start walking again. We were hungry and hadn't eaten since the morning. My boyfriend grabbed some of the corn and shoved it into my backpack. He said we would cook it in the husks over a fire. I was never allowed to cook, so I had no idea if that was possible or not.

The grass on the hill grew taller and more challenging to walk through. We shifted and walked on a road under the stars, ducking in the grass when cars drove by. The night was beautiful. We all talked about what we would do once we got to Texas.

Suddenly, a bright light cut through the night and shined toward us. We scattered. My friends tried to hide in the grass, and my boyfriend pulled me toward the cornfields. I called back to my friends to run, but they were too scared to move. The car stopped on the road near where my friends were hiding. A bright light pierced through the darkness toward them.

I didn't know what was going on, but I couldn't leave them there alone. I started running back. My boyfriend caught my arm.

"They are cops," he said. "They are busted. The cops will take them back home. Leave them. We can still make it."

"I can't just leave them! They are my friends. We should stick together no matter what."

He stood and watched as I walked cautiously back toward the cops and my friends. The bright light found my body as I turned around to see if my boyfriend was following me. All I saw was an empty cornfield.

That night, in the cop car, my friends told me they would have never turned back for me.

The cops took me home last. It was past midnight. When they had dropped off my friends, I went into grave detail about what was happening at home. I told them the pain my father had inflicted on me and begged them to call my mother in Texas or take me anywhere other than home. They said they could not. The law wouldn't allow it. They had to return me to the person who had custody of me.

The officers ushered me into the house, and my parents were silent. One of the officers started to pry some of the things I had said. Hope sparked in my bones again. But my father dodged every accusation with a remark about how uncontrollable I was, skipping school, causing drama at home, and so forth.

The officer walked to me and handed me a card. He whispered, instructing me to call him if anything happened when he left. As they were leaving, they passed my parents, my bookbag exposing corn, which my parents mockingly informed me was for cows, not human consumption.

When the cops left our home, my father took the card. "You don't need this."

MY FATHER STATED he had had enough. He called my mema in Texas and arranged for me to return to Texas for good.

The night before I was to leave, he instructed me to remove my clothes and lay on my bed. His hands held a camera.

"I am not going to let you take naked pictures of me," I said

"Oh, yes, you are. I can't have you going down to Texas and telling everyone I beat you. Now I will have proof I did not."

"This time," I said.

"Off."

"Whatever. By tomorrow, I'll be gone."

He took a few minutes to put me in awkward positions and take many pictures.

"Spread your legs wider. Okay, now get on your knees and face the wall," he instructed. My father's girlfriend was downstairs. I was unsure if she knew his plan to "protect" himself. I secretly hoped someday she would find the pictures and he would be exposed.

When it was finally time to leave, I was elated! Feeling like I had won, we sat outside the bus stop before the first light, waiting for my bus to arrive. It was hard to keep my teenage angst composure while waiting for this epic moment. I was going *home, my home.* This trip would start on one bus, but I would need to transfer a few times before arriving in Texas.

Still, within a few days, I would be back where I belonged.

As I was about to take the bus, my father stood somber next his girlfriend.

"I really do love you," he said. "Be safe. Call if you need anything."

Cell phones were not popular when I was a teenager. Even if they had been, I wouldn't have had one. I hesitated in front of the open door on the bus. I was unable to detect if he was sincere. I could count on one hand how many times he said anything caring in my life. I thought perhaps he realized he would never see me again.

For a moment, I felt sad for him. After all, I was his daughter. But when his girlfriend mewed sadness in support of him, I realized why he had said those words, which had nothing to do with me.

The trip was two days long. I did not have much money, nor did I have food or anything to keep me occupied. But I was well taken care of by strangers. Some saw me traveling alone and took it upon themselves to watch over me, sharing their headphones and food.

I did not feel lonely or uncomfortable. All I could think about was my memories of the previous summer and hope for this new adventure. Life was going to be different, and I couldn't wait to discover how.

When I arrived in Texas, my mother informed me I would be staying with her, not my mema, as they had told my father. I didn't care. I thought it would be fun to live with my mother in the city. We had not spent much time together last summer.

My first night in my mother's apartment was different. She rented a small two-bedroom apartment. The furniture in the living room consisted of a few pop-up chairs and a twenty-inch box TV with two large antennas growing out of the top and wrapped in foil. The TV sat on the floor with pliers acting as a remote. She did not subscribe to cable but could get three channels with the makeshift antenna.

The carpet was an off-white shade, with no vacuum to pull up the accumulated dirt and stains. A square mustard-yellow table occupied the only available corner of our small kitchen. The cupboards were bare of food. My room was also empty upon my arrival.

My mother had her favorite posters, t-shirts, and whatever else tacked to the walls in her room. It reminded me of a teenager's room, and I wondered if it's what my room in Wisconsin would have looked like had I been able to decorate, except with Eminem posters instead of Guns and Roses.

On our very first night together, she made me fried chicken. She told me it was the first meal she made my father and filled my head with some of her good memories from when they first met "before he changed." For a moment, I was a teenage girl who got to hear of how her parents fell in love, and it felt nice.

We did not live in that apartment long. My mother often could not pay the rent due to drug and alcohol abuse, so we hopped from place to place. Her preferences were weed, cocaine, Xanax, Lortabs, beer, and men. She has dabbled with a few others.

Due to a temporary custody letter my father had written, I attended eighth grade at Stroman Middle School in Texas. The letter was not legal, but the school accepted me as a new student. School was not easy. I was a decent student when I wanted to be, but my attitude did not serve me well. You can easily take the girl out of the damage, but it's much more challenging to get the damage out of the girl.

I still struggled with some defensive patterns I developed growing up. I felt like every kid had it out for me. I was still getting into trouble for fighting when I wasn't trying to skip school.

Within my first week of school, I attempted to skip class. I was brought back to school in handcuffs for a B&E. It was an abandoned house. I was not looking to steal anything. I just wanted to hide out until school was over. Because of this, my offense was a misdemeanor and not a felony.

After a fight with one of the other boys during class, a security guard pulled me out into the hall and asked me why I could not get along with the other kids. I told her they picked fights with me. She said she had known these children since they were born, and while they were not perfect, they weren't bullies, as I claimed. Felt pretty typical not having anyone believe me.

I decided to get real when I was let back into the room. I asked the class why they singled me out and made fun of me. The teacher disapproved of my approach, but I told him if I was going to "get over it and move on," then I needed to know why.

We had an honest discussion. The kids did not understand why I didn't want to be in school and why I disrupted class. Showing up to school the first week in handcuffs didn't help. It made me an "easy target." The security guard didn't like that because they had just admitted they were singling me out and purposely picking on me. I shot her a *told you so* glance and kept the conversation going.

They also said I was closed off and unapproachable—always angry.

I did not explain away my behavior. I thanked my

classmates and told them I would try harder. Not try harder to be liked, but try harder to be a good student and not disrupt the class. I understood those kids were not my enemies. Although, at the time, I did not realize who my enemy was or why I wanted so desperately for everyone to hate me and like me at the same time.

I thought the issue was over, but the security guard would not let me avoid her. She was determined to keep me on my new path. I would see her coming toward me down the hall and duck out behind another student.

Finally, she called me to the principal's office. She cornered me and would not let me go until she dug deep enough. I cracked, burst into tears, and told her I had never fit in. I had always struggled in school, not because I didn't understand the material but because I never got along with my class. My father made me feel like an unwanted piece of property, and though I was with my mother, she seemed to be more interested in guys, drugs, and alcohol.

We had a class experiment not too long before the security guard called me to her office. All I needed to bring was an egg. My mother told me we couldn't afford to buy eggs because she planned to sell the rest of her food stamps to get some cash for the bar that night.

I was embarrassed and tried to tell the teacher quietly, but she used me as an example and told the class I came unprepared. Also, she did not think I was telling the truth, so she confronted me in front of my classmates. She refused to start the experiment until I said I did not come prepared and lied about my mother selling the food stamps.

The security guard told me I would not be in pain forever. It was my choice each day to decide who I would be, and she made it mandatory for me to see a counselor/therapist to help me work through my "issues."

I was not pleased with the security guard's orders—I was pissed. But in this school, you did what the guards said or didn't go to school. I had been down this road before. I had talked to someone about my struggles three times, and they made my problem worse each time.

I began to see a therapist through no choice of my own, although I did appreciate skipping class. After a long period of developing a relationship and skirting around my "issues," I shared my first story. My voice started to rise as I broke through the barriers until I was screaming the words out between sobs.

The counselor tried to calm me down, but I screamed until I passed out. I woke up on the floor of the therapist's office, confused. I had never fainted before.

I did not know what was happening to me, and I was petrified. I had never felt so out of control. I started hyperventilating again.

The school had called my mother. We lived right down the street, so she arrived quickly. She gave me a pill to take and told me to breathe. Not long after I took her medication, I felt relaxed. Anytime someone mentioned my father's name, panic would set in so intensely my mother started giving me those little pills to calm me down.

The counselor and I continued to work together. With her help, I gained more confidence and less anger. I started doing better in school, if you consider no longer skipping class a significant improvement.

The therapist discussed with me the protocol for taking my story to court. At first, I was completely against it, but after some thought, I decided I was ready even though I was terrified of my father. I had the support of my mother, family, and counselor, who I had grown to value as part of my tribe. Together they promised I would never have to see him again.

I was sick from the stress often, but I was getting through it. My heart knew I needed to be brave. None of my new friends knew what I was going through. Life went on while the process began. The first step was alerting the courts in Wisconsin of my plan to press charges. I didn't hear anything for a while and continued my therapy, though school would end soon.

On a typical gorgeous Texas day, one call changed everything. I was at my friend's house when my mother came to the door. She had the cordless phone in her hand and said it was for me. (We lived upstairs at the time.)

I wondered who would be calling me. My excitement grew as I snatched up the phone to discover the mystery caller.

I answered the phone. My stomach dropped when I heard his voice on the other end. "Are you alone?" he asked. My head started spinning, my chest felt like lead, and my stomach threatened to release my lunch.

"No," I replied. I looked at my mother, my friend, and her mother. Each of them stared back at me.

I walked into my friend's room. My father told me the cops were staking out his house. He had noticed them for some time and went to confront them on the street. He said the cops informed him I was pressing charges and that they needed to watch his house because children lived there.

I listened to him talk. He was angry and short with his words. I didn't say a word, but my confidence grew while I was on the phone listening to his words.

"What you did to me was wrong!" I interrupted.

"What!? What did I do?"

"You hit me. You touched me. You stalked me! I saw you outside of the school! You followed me when I was babysitting, and then you lied about it! You told [stepmom] that you were going to the store, but you didn't! You were following me!"

I kept going, bringing up details, such as the naked pictures he took, the bathroom, the bedroom, the weight room, the garage, and so forth. I kept going until I was crying. Every word I spoke made me more fearful of his reaction.

Silence.

His tone changed from harsh to soft as if he were trying to comfort me.

"You can't really believe this? I didn't do any of that. I would never hurt you," he said.

"There was no film in the camera. I just wanted you to believe it so you wouldn't say I hit you. And the garage, I was just teaching you how to work out (naked), and I only followed you to make sure you were okay. Listen ..."

He began telling me a story of how he had injured his back so badly he couldn't walk. His new wife had to help him get dressed each day, and he cried over the phone about how embarrassing it was for him. He told me he loved me, and now by pressing charges, I was going to hurt him badly.

His voice echoed through the phone. "The therapist coerced you to further her career, and I will talk to her! And now you want to send me to jail where I won't even be able to walk. I'll get killed in jail. What will my wife think? What about your sister or brother? Who is going to take care of them? You don't want to do this. You got what you wanted. You are far from me in Texas. Why do this?"

I will never forget the word "coerced" because I didn't know what it meant. When I told my father this, he had me grab a pen and paper to write it down so I wouldn't forget how to say it to the therapist.

I wasn't sure what to say. I was hurt, but he had asked some questions I could not answer. Would my brother and sister end up in foster care? Would he die in prison? Was there no film in the camera?

I told him I would drop the charges and hit the off button on the cordless phone.

When I informed the therapist of *my* decision, she was outraged but unwilling to give up. She wasn't mad at me as much as she was upset over his claim that she coerced me.

"What would I have to gain from you sharing your story?"

That's a good question. She made a fine point, and I began to see that my father had manipulated me again.

The therapist was exactly what I needed in my life. She remained supportive and told me I was strong. She said we would still keep talking, and we could continue the process of turning him in again if I felt I was ready. She also scolded my mother for letting him speak to me, which I thoroughly enjoyed watching.

Being in the presence of my therapist made me feel strong. She spoke to my mother in a no-BS kind of way, very matter-of-fact. Her direct nature in calling my mother out on her poor life choices encouraged me to set some boundaries of my own.

However, something shifted in my confidence within a few weeks of my father's phone call. My therapist became shifty, edgy even. Someone canceled my future appointments with her, and the office lady told me I was no longer allowed to see her.

Fear and confusion distracted me from school. I asked my mother, school teachers, and friends what I had done wrong, but no one could answer my questions, and the more I brought it up, the more they seemed annoyed.

I begged to talk to her. I even started skipping class to try to catch her between sessions. I wanted to know why she didn't want to see me. I needed to know if she was angry with me.

I felt weak and disappointed in myself. I figured she didn't like me anymore because I was not strong enough to take my father to court. She must have been so disappointed in me.

While all this was happening, my little sister back home was becoming the same age I was when he started grooming me. The counselor once said an abuser would only stop if he felt fear of being caught or was caught. I was not strong enough to confront my abuser at that time, but I take comfort in thinking my actions may have been what protected my sisters over the years from receiving the same "love" as I did.

The school year ended, and I told myself it was over. At least I wouldn't ever have to return to my father's home, as my mom and the counselor had promised.

Chapter 21

"Every single journey that I've embarked on, I've learned something new."

—SHAILENE WOODLEY

Summer began. As a young teen, that means exploring parties, campfires, and lots of food. Though we often did not have money and moved regularly, I had my family and was happy.

One weekend, my mother was in a motorcycle accident. Overall, she was okay, but she could not drive. We were staying at her friend's house out in the country as we had lost another apartment due to a lack of funds. With each move, we lost more of our belongings. After a while, all we had was what could fit in the van.

There was a boy who lived down the street. He wanted to date me for about five minutes until I told him I thought lighting farts on fire was disgusting, and it was. Totally funny as a friend but not sexy at all.

That boy had a four-wheeler, and we would often ride in the mud with a group of other kids. The girls would scream in panic as dirt flew on their clean clothes. On the other hand, I wanted to drive that four-wheeler and get muddy.

One morning, after much begging, he finally let me drive his pride and joy. I rode around the dirt driveway, which looped around from the road. Endless circles, dodging my mother's parked van—until I didn't.

My mother said she watched the accident in slow motion. I hit a sand hole, going as fast as the wheeler would allow, and it threw the wheeler straight into the van's path. At full force, I hit the vehicle head-on. The hood on the van crunched in. My body started lurching toward the windshield when I felt a strong pair of hands wrap around my waist and pull me back down to the seat. My mother couldn't explain what she saw, but I could. That wasn't the first time I had felt my guardian angel.

However, I didn't *walk* away. The handle of the four-wheeler went into my left leg and required immediate attention. My mother panicked because the hospital was a long way out, and she couldn't drive because she and her friends were high. I finally convinced her that I knew how to drive—how hard could it be?

I drove us safely to the hospital forty minutes away and unknowingly just interviewed to become my mother's new sober driver. I had also inadvertently given my mother the thought that it would benefit me to have a job since I could drive. Don't get my age confused; I was a fresh fourteen. I could drive, but it wasn't legal.

After I healed, my mother had me fill out applications to help provide some income.

A buffet-style restaurant hired me right away. I wanted to be a server, but they felt I was not ready after the interview. They asked me what I would do if a customer said something rude about my bottom while pouring coffee. I told the manager I would pour the coffee onto the customer's lap. So, I worked in the back for a while. It was okay. Lots of folding silverware into uncooperative cheap napkins, stacking glasses, and swapping out food on the buffet.

My mother did not work. She lived off of disability (she was not disabled), food stamps, and alcohol. My mother would drop me off before my shift. She would then go to the bar and drink all day. When my shift was over, she would pick me up from work but would be drunk beyond recognition and slide to the passenger side so I could drive.

I would drive us back to the bar. Occasionally, I would drop her off at the bar and swing home quickly to take a shower. Other times, I would sit in the corner of the bar drinking a beer while waiting for the bar to close.

Sometimes we would play pool, dance, or hang out with her buddies. When the bar closed for the evening, it was time to convince my mother (stubborn as a mule) to enter her almost brakeless, seatless van and get her home—a pretty standard evening.

I had my fair share of fun and reckless nights at underage drinking parties. Texans love to dance, hit the swimming holes, slap the back of a mean bull, and haul ass. I smoked weed and cigarettes and occasionally popped some of my mom's pills. I had her consent. God help anyone crazy enough to steal that woman's drugs. There were few things she cared about more. Some of these were habits I picked up in Wisconsin and were just as easy to resume in Texas. Others I found while in Texas.

I was often conflicted about how I felt regarding my mother. She was not the mother I had envisioned. She taught me street skills—like how to check the purity of cocaine—instead of life skills, like how to pay rent. There were times we didn't have a roof over our heads.

I was embarrassed she was my mother and seemed to have no ambitions, fell into "love" too quickly, and couldn't hold a job. But she was happy, albeit drunk and high every day. She loved her life.

I was not the healthiest kid by any means. I tried to get her to stop doing drugs and go for walks with me, but she always had some excuse. "My ankle twists when I walk, so I can't go for walks," she would say. Her reasons would make me feel resentful.

A few nights after this conversation, she had gotten drunk and was naked, jumping up and down on her bed in her room, screaming. She wanted to see her third, or maybe her fourth, ex-husband. She could jump for him but couldn't walk for me.

Here is how that evening when down.

My mother often looked for love in sex. She felt sex meant she was desired and had control. Her ex, who had her throwing toddler tantrums this evening, left her because she was irresponsible and always drunk or on drugs. She was the same person before he married her, but that was none of my business.

Our apartment had one bedroom, one bath, a small kitchen, and a living room. My mother was in the bedroom, and I slept on a twin mattress on the floor in the living room with barely a sheet to cover me. My mother wasn't trying to neglect me; she "couldn't afford" a lot.

All my work money went to cigarettes, gas, alcohol, and "food" because she sold the food stamps for more alcohol. I couldn't buy something for myself because she felt it was selfish. However, my sister and I occasionally went to the mall and got our nails done. Our mother would find out, but my sister always told her she paid for whatever I bought.

My mother had gotten so drunk that evening that she began jumping up and down on her bed naked, screaming she wanted to see her husband. I explained that he was her ex-husband and wanted nothing to do with her, but that didn't change her mind. She was screaming that life was unfair and no one loved her.

"You don't count!" she said.

She started throwing beer bottles at my head. The bottles crashed against the wall, leaving brown shards of glass on the floor. We did not have a vacuum, so I put my shoes on. She threw another bottle. She couldn't have hit the broadside of a barn if she were standing right in front of it, but she sure could make a mess.

These episodes were becoming more frequent. Many people would ask how this made me feel. There was nothing she did that made me feel worse than what my father did to me.

She jumped off the bed and said she was leaving to get him. She had no intention of getting dressed. It was one in the morning. I was exhausted, but she wouldn't stop screaming and tried to grab the keys to drive to his house, naked. While capturing the keys in my hand, I told her I would go if she promised to put on clothes and stop screaming. As if she were three years old and I had handed her chocolate, she ran back to her room smiling and put on a t-shirt and shorts.

I drove her sixty minutes to her ex-husband's residence. He lived with his mother. We couldn't come into their home, so she convinced him to return to the apartment. By convinced, I mean she started screaming again until he was so afraid his mother would wake up and kick him out that he practically threw her into the van. On the way back, I put earbuds in and hit play on my CD player, thinking they would want privacy to talk. Our stereo didn't work, so I often had earbuds in the car.

When we arrived back at the apartment, I pulled out my earbuds, turned around to tell them we were home, and my mother's bright white bottom was up in the air, searing a picture in my brain I wouldn't wish for anyone to witness. This time I was screaming.

I jumped out of the van, went into the apartment, flipped my bed over so it didn't have glass, and went to bed.

The next morning, I shared my lack of appreciation for her having sex in the van while I was driving.

"Well, you shouldn't have been looking."

Her comment stung. I felt undervalued and disrespected.

The cycle of drugs, alcohol, and moving around continued. My aunt got tired of seeing me in that situation and invited me to stay with her and her family. They had a three-bedroom trailer that was very well-kept and clean. My uncle played the guitar, and my whole family in Texas drank daily, so parties were always going on. As a teen, I loved it.

I had a room at my aunt's house, but I often fell asleep on the couch listening to my uncle and his friends jamming out to Godsmack or Metallica on their guitars and drums. They were highly talented. They could never understand how I would fall asleep with my head next to the drum set, but I understood. I felt safe.

Another summer had gone, and it was time to return to high school. I wanted so badly to go to the same high school as my sister. We talked about it all summer long. She was popular in a no-BS, just-as-tough-as-the-boys way, and I would have big shoes to fill.

Weeks before I was supposed to start, the school called and rejected my paperwork. They did not accept my father's letter to get me into the school and denied my entry.

Technically, my mother did not have custody of me. Because she did not have custody of me, the school would not allow me to attend. When she called my father to explain, he refused to do anything and said I would have to return *home*.

He wanted control again.

Because of Texas law, I needed to go back to Wisconsin. Parents go to jail if the child does not attend school. My mother did not fight for me. She said it would take too much time and money.

"It will only be for about four years, then you will be eighteen, and you will be able to come back," she said.

When I reminded her of her promise, she brushed it off. "We all have to grow up sometime."

Even after everything, all she could say was, "He wouldn't hurt you now that he knows you will tell, and you can come back next summer." It was as if I were four years old, and she was dropping me back off on his doorstep "until next year."

Chapter 22

"Understand that the right to choose your own path is a sacred privilege. Use it. Dwell in possibility."

—OPRAH WINFREY

In Texas, I started the process of filing charges against my father because my mother promised I would be safe from him. Though, the process quickly came to a halt. I thought the "safe from him forever" should still have held true. Yet, I was on my way back to Wisconsin. No one would stand up to him. How could I? Disney taught me the bad guy never wins, but life was teaching me another lesson.

I made the decision I was going to fight back if he dared to touch me. Even though my small punches would feel like a bee sting, I was still going in swinging. I would scream to the high heavens. Or, I would run away for the fourth time. One way or another, I was getting out of there.

Once again, upon my arrival in Wisconsin, I was not allowed to talk to anyone in Texas. My father took my little teenage address book, and I was not allowed to use the phone.

"There is no one for you to call. You don't have any friends, and they obviously don't want you back in Texas," he said

Finding my usual coping vices proved difficult. I would steal cigarettes from my new stepmother but could not find anything else until school started, so I would sneak into the kitchen and eat.

Once school started, I picked up after my mother and began to look for love in all the wrong places. I lived in the drama of teenage angst and made many bad choices— skipping school, drugs, alcohol, etc.

Being back in the same high school was unnerving. I knew many people but didn't finish my first year because I went to Texas. There were many rumors about why I had left, none of which mattered, nor were they correct.

Now a sophomore in high school, I made different friends than I had in my freshman year. I met some new people who quickly became my group. We all had our struggles, and we were all trying to find ourselves, but the memories we created are some I will forever cherish. My sophomore and junior years were spent occasionally working, doing the bare minimum at school, smoking between classes, and being as far away from home as possible.

Along my journey, I met a good friend. She was a fantastic girl with so much love, generosity, and grace.

I remember the first night I went to her parents' house. We were a wee bit drunk, and I saw a kitty on her back porch. Because it was dark out, and perhaps because I was tanked, I didn't notice the screen door separating me from the little kitty. I ran to the cuteness at full force and plowed right through the screen door. That was my introduction to her incredibly forgiving parents.

I remember being terrified that her father would yell at

me and then call my dad, who would do something much worse, but he just laughed and said, "The door can be replaced; you can't."

When I had grown up a bit, I realized what a great friend I had and tried like hell to find her. I had lost contact with her when she went to college. I missed her so much that I attempted to track her down in Paris! I never did find her and tell her how thankful I was for her friendship.

My father had not tried any of his old tricks after my return. He still yelled a lot, but his ability to cause physical harm was difficult with the new spirits occupying our house. There were more words than fists. Kicking me out of the house was becoming a norm, but I would eventually end up back home as I had nowhere to go.

When my freedom finally came at seventeen, I welcomed it with the clothes on my back and nothing else. I told my father I was going to stay with a friend and would never be returning home.

"Don't come crawling back when they kick you out, too," he responded.

No one—not my mother, father, or even school—prepped me for adulting's enormous responsibilities. Money was the hardest. No one taught me how to save, spend, and do everything in between. At this point, I wasn't even living paycheck to paycheck. I was underage, living on the streets, sleeping on friends' couches, and dining at the local free eats, including churches, The Salvation Army, and other food pantries.

I was unreliable, irresponsible, and soaked in shenanigans.

I worked at a few places and managed to rent once I had turned eighteen, but I never stayed anywhere longer than a few months. The boss, the manager, my teacher, and the landlord (fill in the blank) were always "an asshole." My problems seemed to be everyone else's fault but my own. When my friends wanted me to take responsibility for myself, I viewed it as abandonment.

During the end of my senior year, I was diagnosed with mononucleosis, and my school would not let me come to school or take my exams. Due to my past attendance and overall grades, I was encouraged to drop out and come back to repeat my senior year. I would not be walking with the rest of my class, but the impact of my decisions did not bother me at the time.

I dropped out.

Moving, partying, and boys had become my oasis for a few years. But I grew tired of my method of survival. I felt lonely, hopeless, broken, and hated. There was nowhere for me to go anymore. Not long before I turned nineteen, I walked through the doors of The Salvation Army, asking for help.

First, I want to say how thankful I am for The Salvation Army. They provided shelter, food, necessary supplies, kind staff, and encouragement for a better path.

There was no extra space in the shelter. There were, at times, five people in a tiny room. The smell of accumulated farts was intense, and the packaged food was always past its due date. This isn't a jab toward The Salvation Army; it's a cry for our community to come together and make a change because I would not be where I am today without them.

There were two types of people in The SA: people who needed a break and wanted to be on their feet and people looking for a handout. Some folks were so scared to go out to try and fail that they wouldn't even try. Before moving into The Salvation Army, I had been the person looking for a handout who didn't know what I needed was a break.

I needed a place to feel safe to reflect on where I was and where I wanted to be. I wanted to learn how to be self-sufficient, build strong relationships, travel, and more. I didn't want to end up like my mother, and I was on the fast track to her lifestyle. My father kept a nice home and a job, but I also did not want to become him, what I perceived as an empty shell devoid of any real connection.

On a Sunday morning, my other SA roommates gathered around to watch *Lord of the Rings* on a small box TV. I watched them instead of the movie. I wondered how they could feel so comfortable living in this space. Some were content with not looking for a job or a place to live. They thought they had everything they needed here.

Or maybe they were just exhausted from always fighting through life. I got that. Even at my young age, it felt like every day for as long as I could remember was a fight. I wondered if life would always feel this way, and if so, would I eventually give up too?

When it came to The SA, you could always tell who would make it out of the system and who would be a lifer. The lifers had given up. Maybe circumstances beat them down. Perhaps they never took responsibility for themselves. I don't know. I know everyone had a story, and once you heard it, you understood how they ended up in the struggle. It was no excuse, just an understanding.

So many people fail at life because they don't understand the rules of the game. My rule had always been to keep fighting, and I was starting to think I was not playing the right game. For years I swung at everything and everyone, and now I was alone.

Before I could figure out what I would do, someone

offered me a couch. I was prideful, entitled even. I didn't think someone like me belonged in The Salvation Army, so I left quickly, no different than the girl who had walked through their door a few weeks back.

I stayed at my new friend's apartment for some time.

As I previously mentioned, I did not understand money and responsibility and will openly say I did not understand friendship. I met many amazing people mixed with not-so-amazing people, but I struggled to tell the difference and treated them the same. I also still had no sense of responsibility. Eventually, my roommate tired of my attitude about life, and I was bouncing from couch to couch again.

I ended up back in The Salvation Army for another round. This grace is why The Salvation Army is dear to my heart. I was at rock bottom, still swinging at the air. I didn't know where to throw punches to impact my life in a way that would stick. I had yet to do anything different to educate myself on the world. Just simply thinking I would be better wasn't getting me the results. I needed a plan, so I went to the front desk to see if they could help.

"I need to get out of this place."

"Excuse me?" the front staff cocked her head to the side with an attitude caused by my ungrateful statement.

"No, no, sorry. That's not what I mean. I need to be better; I can be better," I corrected myself quickly. I wasn't winning friends here either.

"Go see the receptionist in the front office."

I smiled and nodded, hoping I didn't just make more issues for myself.

The receptionist set up an appointment for me to talk to an advisory counselor to discover what my first step would be. I was anxious about the meeting. I felt hope for the first time. I kept thinking about what she might say.

The counselor talked to me about getting my high school diploma.

My chest deflated. "School? That's the best you got?"

She painted a picture of how my life would be easier if I finished school. I could get a better job, rent an apartment, and create something they called a credit score.

The next day I strolled into the school counselor's office and told her of my plan. She paused for a very long minute. She was suddenly staring at me as if I had come in with a face covered in mud. I felt judged and could feel my defensive attitude getting hot. She checked her computer, played with her calculator, and looked back up at me, then back at her computer. The typing of her keys cut through the thick air developing between us.

"There are only six weeks left this year, and you need too many credits. There is no way you can accomplish this."

I was about to spit back some words when I noticed something growing inside me. *She doesn't think I can do this? Maybe I can't. I am so damn sick of people telling me what I can and can't do!*

I had nothing going for me—no friends, no home, no purpose. I had no job and couldn't get one without my diploma. I could work day and night catching up on the homework, and that's precisely what I would do.

I looked her dead in the eye and said, "I can do this, but if I can't, then I fail another year. If I can, then it would be one hell of a story, wouldn't it?"

Her eyebrows went up, and she smiled.

"Yes, it would. I hope you do. I guess we'll see you Monday."

I smiled, finished the paperwork, and left with more

excitement than I could handle. I ran back to the counselor and told her my good news. Like a good parent, she said, "Great! Now get to work." It was a little deflating, but she was right. It was time to get to work.

To the disbelief of the students, teachers, and administration (but not The Salvation Army), I did finish school. I received my diploma on May 17, 2004, and I was so proud.

And that's when my life became easy, and all my dreams came true (insert laughing emoji).

I had hit the target, but the magical doors to my new life were not opening fast. No one was chasing me down with unique opportunities. I did manage to find a job. After a while, a new friend offered to have me as a roommate.

It was time for me to leave The Salvation Army, but I was scared. Could I stand on my new wobbly legs? The staff could see I was ready, but my knees felt like someone had replaced them with jello.

To help me move on, one of the staff gave me a quilt. This was a big deal. While staying, we were only allowed one blanket. I think I was born unable to regulate my body temperature because I am always cold. One night a staff member took pity on me and gave me an extra blanket. I had to hide it while I was there.

Another rule was that we were not allowed to take the pillows, blankets, sheets, etc., with us when we left. So, a staff member handing me my blankie when I left was a huge deal.

Seventeen years later, that blanket still sits on my bed. It reminds me constantly of my perseverance and the importance of giving someone a second chance. I do what

I can to help The Salvation Army and food pantries so when another Niki walks through the door, they will have the tools they need to help her.

Chapter 23

"The world I left always finds a way to reel me back in."

—J.D. VANCE

I wish I could say I had it all figured out the second time I left The Salvation Army. What I lacked in skill, I made up for in determination. I struggled with controlling my emotions, taking responsibility, being a good friend, and so forth.

Again, I met some generous souls who helped me along the way. I also met some people who were struggling more than me. I felt torn between the two. I never felt like I was good enough or worthy of the friendship of the "good influences," and the "bad influences" seemed to accept me for who I was, which was a nice change of pace.

I am not referring to judging people as good vs. evil. I'm talking about the pull from a life of peace vs. the life of drama, drugs, violence, and cops. Sometimes your lessons are learned from what you don't want in your life.

I had a tough time discovering and reaching who I wanted to be but knew exactly who I wasn't. And yet, my family's mannerisms seemed to leak out of me and poison the ground from which I was working so hard to grow fruit.

I disappointed my friends, looked for love in the wrong places, bounced jobs, etc. I was making progress, but it would be a few years before my newly planted seeds would grow and bloom.

The nightmares in my father's home were no longer my life. I had not spoken to my father and had no intention of ever speaking to him again. When I shared my story with others, their first question was, how did my father come back into my life? Perhaps you can make sense of this because I have no idea what happened to this day. Was it God's plan, or was someone else controlling the marionette strings?

It was warm outside, and fall was beginning to arrive. The change in weather painted the ground with fallen leaves. Our apartment did not have air conditioning, so the cooler weather felt nice. I watched the people walking by on the sidewalk while inhaling my cigarette, lost in thought.

A cop pulled up at my home. I had no reason to worry. Those old days were behind me.

"Niki?"

Panic and hesitation came over me immediately.

"Yes, that's me."

"You have a warrant out for your arrest."

"Oh no, I don't. I haven't done anything wrong—no tickets, no trouble."

My legs were prepared to sprint. I If I ran through the front door, I could slow him down and get out the back. But where would I go? And besides, I had no reason to run.

Yes, I had a history with cops, and I had been in jail for an underage drinking ticket for a few days—they'd said I'd be back. I was not on cloud nine just yet, but I was starting to understand how the world worked, and I kept my nose out of trouble. He had no reason to arrest me. I thought my innocence would be enough to sort it all out.

"No, officer, I know I do not have a warrant," I repeated as my head shook from side to side.

"You do, and I am going to need you to come with me."

The cop would not tell me the warrant. He said he didn't know and needed to take me to the station to sort it out. My emotions went into overdrive. *I will never be free; this will be my life forever. Scared of the cops, jumping from place to place, never keeping a job. This world is fucking impossible.*

I stubbornly refused to leave with him, and eventually, he told me I had a ticket due that was over $450, and if I could find the money, he wouldn't take me in. He refused to tell me what the ticket involved. He acted as though he was irritated he was doing me a favor by giving me time to come up with the cash.

I could not get the money, and I certainly didn't have it, so he arrested me and booked me.

The holding cells were six-by-eight feet with no window and a solid door providing a little slot just large enough for food. There was no daylight, no clock, no magazines, a cold metal silver toilet in the corner, and a small green mat for sleeping.

Time was irrelevant. I was alone, confused, and trapped, and no one would tell me what was happening. I started losing my mind, and I wasn't the only one.

Another girl beat me to my sanity loss. She started shrieking from her cell, and I can only assume she was slamming her head and fists into the wall. I peered from my small food slot in the door and watched the guards try to rush through a few closed metal gates to get to her door.

By the time the guards got to her cell, she was silent. They called for a medic and took her out of the cell, covering her body. She was unconscious. I never saw the girl, but I could see the blood on the floor and the inner door when they swung it open. A guard's face twisted in sadness and pain as he shook his head from side to side. The fear of that moment brought me back. For the rest of my time in the cell, I sang Men at Work's "Who Can It Be Now" over and over until they came to let me out a couple of days later.

It seemed an eternity had passed when they came to put me in a different cell. A guard handed me a stiff blue set of clothes, and they gave me shoes. I was walked down a white hall smelling of pungent cleaner to another jail area where I would have roommates.

We each had a cell, and I had three other roommates. A TV hung on the wall behind bars. Some worn books sat on a metal picnic table, and there was a pay phone and one shower (with limits of use), and still no ability to look outside.

I was crying uncontrollably, totally helpless. I couldn't fight what I couldn't see, and no one seemed to know why I was in there, but apparently, it was none of my business. At first, my cellmates mocked me.

"Yeah, I don't deserve to be in here either"—total cliché. But eventually, one of them believed I did not know why I was in jail or when I was getting out. She had a plan. She had found a way to call people and leave messages without money. Do you remember collect calls, "wehadababyitsaboy"? (Ask your parents. You may even need to go back further and ask your grandparents.)

She asked me about my mom or dad. "Nope, not happening," I told her. My father was out of my life, and I did not want to see him again. With a stern, matter-of-fact tone, she convinced me it was my best shot. She called and left a voice message claiming she was the Clerk of Courts, I was an inmate, and my father needed to contact the county immediately to discuss my arrest.

My father did call. According to him, they told him there was no record or reason for me to be in jail, and the next day I was released into his custody. Why into his custody? I don't know. I was twenty years old. I contacted the Clerk of Courts—no apology for the arrest, no payment for wages loss.

"The cop was just doing his job and made a mistake," the lady behind the marble countertop stated.

I was back to feeling like life happens to you no matter what you do. To add injury to insult, On September 10, 2004, I had to pay a jail confinement fee of fifty dollars.

I hear you. Why didn't you fight harder? I have pondered that question myself. Picture a young woman with a small record, a history of being seen in the wrong parts of town, no job, no steady living space, and have her stand in front of a judge and tell him an upstanding cop had wrongfully arrested her. Even if they did believe me, what would they have done?

Please do not read into what I am not writing. I am not saying, nor do I believe cops (as a whole) are bad. I am thankful for their service. They see and do a lot to protect us. Most choose to be a cop because they want to help people. If I had been on the right path to start, I'd bet I would have gone into that line of work. I would have made a damn fine detective.

But no matter how many times I spin the wheel, there seems to be no reasonable explanation for my experience.

My father had never picked me up from school on

the coldest winter days, yet he'd picked me up from the courthouse even though I lived three blocks away. I felt something off about the whole event.

When I asked his opinion of the situation, he told me it wasn't worth the time to confront the officer. I felt like he was somehow involved, but the thought of him orchestrating this seemed overly paranoid, and I didn't have any proof.

He pulled up along the curb, crunching the leaves under the tires. I mumbled a thank you and jerked at the handle of his vehicle with no intention of ever seeing him again.

"Niki, wait."

The van was still running as we sat outside my apartment.

He spoke softly. "I don't understand why you won't stop at the house. You have a family who loves you. [Stepmother] asks about you, your brother and sisters...."

I interrupted. "Then why didn't you ever help me when I needed it? Why did you hurt me?" Our dialog continued but went nowhere—the same CD on repeat, scratches and all.

He never took responsibility for his actions. Instead, he told me about his good life and how he wanted me to be a part of it. I missed my sisters and my brother something fierce. They were all growing up without me. None of my high school friends seemed to want me around. A feeling of loneliness crept inside me as he spoke.

I was tired of running, failing, and losing. I worked hard to better my life and still ended up in jail. I felt I had nothing going for me. Except for the abuse from one man, my family was everything to me, especially my sisters and my brother. Was it worth not seeing them so I didn't have to see him? Was it fair to them?

I always carried a romanticized idea of what a family should be. Always together, a love deeper than anything, trust. I wanted someone to be proud of me, have my back, and believe in me. But could we ever be that family?

As I got out of the van, I told him I would stop by the house later that week, and I did.

NOTHING MEANT MORE to me than the idea of being a real family. I played the good daughter as best as possible to win their acceptance and love. Every gold star I received was a sign that I could have the family I thought existed beyond the movies.

Over time, my stepmother's mother helped me find an apartment, taught me how to budget, and helped me buy my first car, a tan '92 Toyota Corolla. It was amazing! I learned how to change a tire and oil.

My apartment was tiny, probably about the size of your living room, but it was MY apartment. The bathroom had only a standing shower and a toilet. The sink was outside the door (in the kitchen) because there was no room in the bathroom. My room was one step away from the bathroom sink (literally) and was too small for a full-size mattress. On the other side of the kitchen were the living room and front door, with just enough room for a futon, small TV, and a plant. Every time I wrote out my check for rent, I was glad I had a place to call my own.

THE HOLIDAYS WERE special to me. It was the time when all of the family would get together. There was always good food, usually a movie on the TV, candy or presents at every gathering, but most of all, there was history. Everyone in the room was a part of a bigger picture. There were old memories and untold secrets shared between members.

But at this time in my life, I hit my target. I had everything I dreamt of when I was living in The Salvation Army. I had a job, an apartment, a family, and friends.

I had a chance.

I was still on my training wheels, a young twenty-one-year-old, but I was improving at balancing and could get from point A to point B.

Everything was precisely as I had thought it should be.

That is until the fantasy I clung to was confronted with the reality that love cannot be built on a foundation of lies.

Chapter 24

"Sometimes our light goes out but is blown into flame by another human being."

—ALBERT SCHWEITZER

S till believing my life was one of the fairy tales, I went on about my day searching and hoping to find the thing that would declare me a "mature adult." I was holding down an apartment and a job. I couldn't cook to save my life, so I lived off fast food and family restaurants. This way of living left my fridge bare, and I received a lot of scrutiny for that, but there were no apparent signs of what I could do so that my family would finally see me as a proud member of society.

The next thing in line was to get married and have kids. At least, that was what it seemed to me to be the next step in becoming an adult. It didn't matter if you liked the guy, as long as your family did. It's sad thinking back that I would have gotten married to make my family happy without even asking myself what I wanted.

But then something magical happened. It's a fairy tale, right?

I was working in a factory. My day-to-day wear was jeans, steel-toe boots, a dirty shirt, and a messy bun. As with every factory, there are office workers, or salary some would call them. They were usually dressed nicely and made way more money than we could imagine. They also went to college and worked their butts off to get there, but we didn't focus on that.

We'd make highly inappropriate sexual jokes and fantasize about what it would be like to date an office "hottie" while the men who worked beside us complained those hotties just had to "sit on their ass in an air conditioned office." If you have ever worked in a factory, you have had this conversation.

Still, it was fun to pretend for a moment that we stood a chance of getting the attention of the cute eye candy that brightened our daily grind.

However, I started to struggle because I didn't see why they couldn't talk to these guys if they were what these girls wanted. They were just people.

Fed up with the constant talk and no action, I decided to prove it was not hard to ask someone out. The rejection would sting a little, but it was expected, so why not just do it!?

There was one guy, in particular, I had my sights on for a long time. His eyes were as blue as the sky on my favorite day. When he would smile, I would melt, though I was always sure he was smiling at someone behind me. He was tall with light brown hair, and the way his jeans hung on his hips, just wow. Magic.

One day, as we girls were "working" (chatting), that boy started walking our way. It was time to prove I had what it took and would do what I said I could.

I lifted my head high and started marching. Butterflies took over my stomach. I could see the girls' eyes getting wider in my peripheral vision. Their hands moved closer to covering their mouths in disbelief. Whispers escaped from their lips.

"Is she really going to do it?"

"She is crazy!"

"No way. This hurts just to watch!"

"Hey!" I said, now just a few feet away from my target.

He smiled and coolly replied, "Hey."

I paused, suddenly forgetting my line was next. I didn't even know what to say.

"So, I was wondering if you would like to come and play some video games later? I have a new system and don't know how to set it up. I figured you're an engineer. Maybe you'd know," I asked.

And then, thinking I sounded lame, I spun on my heel and started walking away. As far as I was concerned, the rejection could happen without me. My grin stretched my face, though, as I gave the girls a look that told them I was fearless and a total badass. Who cared that he thought I was crazy? Most people did, anyway.

"Yeah, that sounds good," I hear from behind me.

Now, with a good chunk of space between us in a loud work area, I stopped in my tracks. My jaw dropped as my head swung back around.

"I'm sorry, what?" I said.

"I said yes. I have been trying to speak to you for a while. You are not an easy girl to talk to. What time should I come over."

I stared at him in disbelief. All of my goofiness and confidence were gone. I gave him the details in a low, slow tone, and he walked away, still grinning.

The girls rushed over to me, and squeals and squeaks echoed around me.

"See?" I said. "No big deal," while trying to catch my breath.

The rest of the day, I was terrified. Was he going to stand me up or set me up?

He showed up that night and found the PlayStation hooked up just fine.

I smiled. "It wasn't hard to figure out the white cord went with the white, the red with the red, and the yellow with the yellow."

"I thought you were smarter than you led on."

We ordered food, played video games, and hung out with my kitties Ashby and Ocean. That was our first date.

THAT HANDSOME MAN and I dated for almost a year when things began to shift.

He broke up with me.

"I care about you, but you are not responsible. You can't take care of yourself. If I am in a relationship with someone, I need to know I can trust them, and I am just not sure I can trust you. I'm sorry."

He wasn't referring to trust in the cheating sense. He meant he needed to rely on us growing as a couple.

The breakup crushed me. It forced me to take an honest, hard look at myself. When I did, I realized there was overwhelming work to be done, and I still didn't know the half of it. I had just been fooling myself.

For starters, I was falling back into some old habits. I left the company I was working for and started job-hopping again. Most of the time, I worked three jobs at once and was damn good at anything I took on. The problem was I was never satisfied. I would work my tail off, but when I got bored, I'd move on.

I was still in party mode, spending my money, drinking and eating my emotions, and drama was everywhere I turned up. I had brought this lifestyle into our relationship, and he wasn't about that life. The more I thought about it, the more I realized I was becoming my mother.

It was time to aim at a target again.

First, keeping a job, paying off old debt, and accepting responsibility.

After a few months, I won him back. It was not easy, but it was so worth it.

I didn't change myself to be with him. I want to make that clear. You should never change WHO you are to be with someone. I did, however, realize that he deserved better, and so did I. I deserved better from myself.

I LOVED WHO I WAS becoming with Lance. I no longer wanted to go out to the bars at night. I wanted to go hiking and fishing. We started camping and traveling. We bought our first house, and I started looking into going to college. Life was not only livable; it was enjoyable.

But something still wasn't right.

My life was the best it had ever been, but I was becoming bitter, resentful, angry, and defensive instead of peaceful or happy. I still felt a demon inside me wanting to break free.

My dear, sweet boyfriend did not know at that time what dark nightmares kept me up at night. He had not seen this kind of anger in someone before and had no tools for how to respond.

I was so mad at myself because I thought I would lose everything I had worked so hard to build if I could not keep it together. I didn't understand why I just couldn't be happy. It was a question I asked myself often.

My father and I had built somewhat of a relationship—primarily superficial. He pretended to care. I pretended my memories were someone else's nightmare. I was getting closer to my family, as I had wanted. I enrolled in college, worked the night shifts, and started going on adventures. I even had a checkbook! I was *happy*. Or so I kept telling myself as I'd reach for one more cookie, one more chip, one more slice of pizza, or one more shot.

Through the few years of overwhelming happiness, I gained much weight. My highest recorded weight was 248, and I bet I had at least forty more pounds. My health was deteriorating fast, and I was only twenty-five!

I was not ready to face the truth, and because of that, my body changed.

I remember the day my health took a hard turn. I was pheasant hunting, and I felt a sharp pain in my stomach and pressure building up in my colon that felt like a rocket about to launch. I started sweating through my hunting clothes, gloved fingers fumbling with my buttons. My bottom barely made it to total exposure before the rocket launched.

Figuring it was something I ate, I didn't put much thought into it—until it happened again the next time I had to go to the bathroom. And again, every day for over a year and a half.

I started to develop a fear of leaving my home. I had a daily forty-minute, bathroom-free country ride to class. I began to avoid football parties (sixteen people, one bathroom), outdoor activities, concerts, travel, large stores—basically any place where I could not map out a bathroom I could get to within seconds.

Not only was I trying to swallow my anger, but I was trying to keep my body from purging anything I ate.

This experience forced me to look inward at my health, though I had no idea where to start. I finally went to the doctor, who referred me to gastroenterology. I tried all their special diets, medication, and ideas for the first year and finished with a colonoscopy. I was getting worse, and they had no answers. The doctors found no solid connection explaining my extreme symptoms.

I started shifting my attention in school and began taking psychology and nutrition classes. Both subjects proved challenging to accept. Soda is terrible for you!? Processed food contains what? Psychopaths, sociopaths, gaslighting, oh my! As I tried to hold on, my head spun but ultimately emerged in learning more about my mind and body.

Meanwhile, my anger and resentment were growing in the darkness, but it was still toward me! I had everything I wanted, everything I had worked so hard to achieve. What else did I need? I felt like an ungrateful brat and was so upset I couldn't get my shit together.

Through all this going on, I got married to that amazing man. He was the only thing I knew I wanted in my life, without a doubt.

As I continued my journey toward a healthier life, the final piece of the puzzle fell in. Words formed sentences about secrets I had long kept. When I drank, little bits of my childhood fell out of my mouth until one night, in a fit of rage, hatred, and a heavy splash of alcohol, my story poured out of me and left my husband speechless. I had kept my secret from him for six years.

He knew our family was somewhat dysfunctional, but he had no idea what kind of secrets I buried inside. He was incredibly supportive by listening whenever I had a breakdown, which happened more often, usually after I visited my father's house. Once the first secret slipped from my heart's cracked foundation, the rest seemed to pour out.

One thing I didn't realize was that my husband would then take on the pain I was releasing. It felt so good to get it out, and no one had ever taken on my pain, so the thought never crossed my mind.

At first, I felt horrible for showing my husband my world because now he was hurting too. After some time, I realized we want to protect our loved ones from the pain, so we hold everything inside. But the truth is, we have to change to hold it in. We have to become darker inside and hide certain parts of us. Doing this hurts our partners, too, because they cannot connect with us fully.

Sharing what aches in our hearts makes it lighter for them and us. They begin to understand why we act the way we do and finally feel they can comfort us. When you have someone who loves you, as my husband does me, they can tell when something inside you is off.

There were more struggles he would face. It hurt his heart to know the woman he loved had experienced something unimaginable. He had to process all of this while working in the same building as my father. He had to look at the man who did those things to me and hold back the anger he now felt.

He knew it was my journey, that he would be my foundation, holding me up so I could stand tall through all the different battles I would face. He knew losing himself, losing his anger, would not help me in any way. He was strong, and with that strength, he made me strong.

That is what a relationship is supposed to be.

I KEPT ON MY JOURNEY of self-discovery and healing as years passed, and it led me to a weight loss workshop. I had made good progress but was stuck and looking to level up.

In this workshop, the leader had us hold a mirror to our faces and tell ourselves we loved ourselves. After mocking his request and getting a good laugh from the others who attended, I held the mirror to my face.

My face did not match what my third eye saw. Looking back was not a girl who loved herself. As if his mirror had some magic power to expose the darkness in my soul, I burst into a flood of salty sadness. *Love me? I am disgusting. I am a coward. I have no talent. Love me? How could anyone love this? But I show so much confidence. I'm funny, or are they laughing at me? It's true, I make many mistakes, but doesn't everyone? Probably not as many as I create.*

I was beginning to understand. The fat around my waist was my way of protecting myself, which was ironic because deep inside, a piece of me hated myself. Why would I protect something I didn't care for?

Over my years of trying to grow as a person, I learned success leaves clues. I followed the clues as well as possible, knowing what I could handle and applying it, starting with food. I realized food could be my slowest poison or my best medicine. My journey would prove to be a long one. I used to eat two Whoppers at a time. I wanted to get to the point of never wanting to eat one Whopper. It's been over seven years since I've had a Whopper or other fast food.

I learned how to read labels, what to eat, and who supplied my food. I was so obsessed with good health I eventually became a specialist in fitness nutrition. Once again, life was moving in the right direction. I followed my path and was surrounded by inspiring people at the level I wanted to be. I had been working on myself for years, continually challenging myself to reach new heights. I was proud of who I had become.

But I was STILL missing something, and the day I admitted this to myself was when God revealed the epic bull's-eye I had unknowingly been training to hit.

I was thirty-two years old. Lance and I had been married for five years. The date was September 27, 2017. I remember it because it was my grandmother's birthday. I had filled out the application, and a few days later, I was at a Boys and Girls Club interviewing to become a "big sister."

My interviewer told me I would be a big sister to a young girl. We laughed and joked around with some of her legal questions. All was good, and then she said, "I just have one more question. Is there anyone in your life you wouldn't want around your little sister?"

The room faded into darkness. My body stayed, but my consciousness lifted to another world where I could feel him touching me. I could smell his breath. I could hear his gasps in my ear. What was only a moment felt like an eternity in the dark. My heart fluttered as though it was under attack. My lungs collapsed as flashes of childhood flipped through my mind like a janky movie reel.

I was a young girl at that moment, drowning in a thick black sludge. The movie reel cut to the future. I pictured him touching my daughter. My hand slid over my stomach as if to protect my bun not yet growing in my oven. *Had he touched my sisters? Did he hurt my brother? How many children has he hurt? How could I continue to be a part of the family and never let my child sleep at their grandparents' house? What excuse will I come up with every time they ask if she can sleep over? Oh no! What about my sisters' kids!? My brother's!?*

My awareness came back into the room. I looked at the worker and said, "No, there is no one in my life I wouldn't want my little to be around." I knew what I had to do. I had to confront my father. It was time to tell my family the truth. I needed them to understand what he was capable of doing. Even if doing so meant it could destroy "my perfect life."

Chapter 25

"No one saves us but ourselves. No one can, and no one may. We ourselves must walk the path."

—BUDDHA

While I wished I was strong enough to stroll into my father's house and confront him once and for all, I did not. The anticipation, fear, and overthinking paralyzed me. My big move was that I stopped contacting him. It seemed like an excellent way to end our "relationship." Not once had he ever called me to see how I was doing or stopped by our home to say hi, so I figured he would fade from my life.

God wasn't on board with my plan.

On October 31, 2017, my phone dinged, indicating I had received a text. I was on my way to work and had just pulled into the parking lot. I parked my car and casually looked down at my phone. There was his avatar staring back at me, and my heart dropped.

Before I read the text, I gave myself a little pep talk that it was probably nothing and could likely ignore it.

I looked down at my phone.

"How's everything going? I don't hear from you. Are you upset with me?"

A sickness filled my belly, and I was overcome with dread. I got out of the car and headed toward the office.

*Do I text him back? Ignore him? Suggest a sit-down conversation and demand he apologizes? The only question I ever wanted to be answered from him was, how? "How could you hurt me so much?" Why could he not have admitted what he did and apologized the many times I confronted him as a kid? We wouldn't be in this position right now. What is his wife going to say? I don't want to hurt her, and what about my family?*My feet spun around, and I headed back toward my car. Knowing I could not leave work, I spun around again and headed back toward the office. I wasn't ready to go in, so I turned back to my car, pacing back and forth in front of the door, clearly unable to make a choice. My stomach twisted tighter. I started to feel dizzy, and my body began to shake. I had strong urges to lie down and start running simultaneously.

It was strange for him to ask if I was upset with him. I had shown no reason for concern before I decided to remove him from my life. I had told no one he knew of my escape plans, if you call it that. He and I had never had a deep, meaningful conversation about anything. This text was out of character.

My head spun out more questions than answers. I knew I had to confront him, but I didn't want anyone else to get hurt. I knew exposing my demons would impact people I cared about deeply. I pictured their faces and imagined their pain for what I was about to do. My throat felt tight. Once I do this, there will be no turning back. Can I do this?

I walked into the building toward my office. Closing my

office door behind me, I continued to pace back and forth. *I have to do this. I want a family. He can't be alone with my children. What if my sisters have kids!? They have to know what he is capable of. What if my brother has kids? What will those kids go through? It will be my fault if anything happens to them. I could have warned them.*

My boss opened the door, took one look at my face, and asked what was wrong. He knew everything about my journey—he was the man who had given me the mirror years prior. The last time we talked, I told him I could no longer have my father in my life, so he knew about that too.

"I don't know if I can do this," I said.

"Do what?"

"It's him. He texted me. He is asking why I haven't contacted him."

"You've got this. You are not the same girl anymore. You are strong. Come to the meeting when you are ready." He closed the door behind him.

I took a deep breath and replied to my father's text.

Me: "I have been in a bad place. I can't keep pretending all the horrible childhood things you did to me didn't happen. I cannot have you as a part of my present or future life. I am not going to start any drama in your life, but I do not want any more contact with you." *Send*

A flood of emotions released from my body as I fell to the floor uncontrollably sobbing. Like a raging river flowing through my body, I let old feelings back in and let them all go simultaneously.

I felt betrayed by my father. He was supposed to protect me, love me, make me strong, and prep me for the evils of this world. He was not supposed to be the biggest evil I would face. He didn't protect me, so now I was going to have to defend myself.

Dad: "That really hurt. Can you and I sit down and talk? If you want me out of your life after that, then so be it. Please."

I knew right away his goal was to manipulate me into silence once more. This was his pattern. He would sit me down, say nice things like he was proud of me, loved me, and then throw in how hard life was for him until I would feel like I was the better person for keeping my mouth shut. He would make me feel like a protector. By keeping our secret, I was protecting my sisters, my brother, and his wife. Carefully, he would switch words around until I could no longer process them, leaving me confused.

Not this time.

My emotion switched, and suddenly I was rageful. "That really hurt." The sentence repeated in my head again and again. A flame lit inside me, and my blood began to boil. *Are you frickin' kidding me? You've got to be fucking joking! That really hurt!? I hurt you!? How do you think I have felt my whole life!? Everything you did to me! Years of feeling your meaty hands pulling my hair as you dragged me through the house, forcing me naked, and making everyone believe I was a horrible kid.*

As upset as I was, I knew I had to tread carefully. If my father goaded me into a fight, it would end badly for me. He was quick to turn a story around to fit his agenda, and all I wanted was for him to be gone and for my healing process to begin.

Me: "No, not right now. There is too much pain. I've been having night terrors and debilitating anxiety attacks. It's affecting every aspect of my life. I need to heal. I won't be around for the holidays. I've just been telling everyone I am busy." *Send*

As far as I was concerned, the conversation was over.

I wasn't sure what would happen next. Would he explain to the family why I was no longer coming around? I knew he would never tell everyone what he had done.

And he didn't.

Instead, he put on a show. He cried to the family and mentioned things like he was a bad father to me and somehow brought blame to my birth mother as if she had anything to do with my decision.

At this point, it had been four years since I had talked to my mother. I had set boundaries, and she would not, or could not respect them. I gave her many chances, but in the end, I had to say goodbye and remove her from my life.

He told his story. The problem was, it wasn't anywhere near the truth.

Now I was the bad guy. I expected family members to reach out and say hurtful things or supportive words.

Crickets. I had to come to terms with the fact that people will believe what they want. I decided I would rather they know the truth and hate me for sharing it than continue to love a version of me I created to protect something evil.

Most of all, I just wanted to get to a place where I could love myself. Life has taught me a valuable lesson: If you can't love yourself, you can't love another, and I wanted to be loved.

"In order to escape accountability for his crimes, the perpetrator does everything in his power to promote forgetting. If secrecy fails, the perpetrator attacks the credibility of his victim. If he cannot silence her absolutely, he tries to make sure no one listens."

—JUDITH LEWIS HERMAN

IT HAS BEEN FIVE YEARS since I told my father I would no longer protect his secret. It was my secret for the longest time, but it was never mine to hold.

I still care about my family. People essential to my heart will someday know the truth. Maybe it was my duty to sit them down and tell them first. I apologize if it was my responsibility to speak to them individually. I had never been in this territory, and as you read many times before, I had told my story to no avail. I did the best I could with what I had.

Being forgotten was not expected, and the abandonment hurt, but I'm sure God heard conversations I didn't and felt certain people weren't good for me at the time of my healing.

Relationships can mend. I discovered many years later that my first stepmother fought for me. She wanted to have me during the weeks she was with my brother and sister. I learned her side of the family, the ones I grew up with, missed me and didn't abandon me as my father told me.

I was loved, and I am betting you are too.

I am proud of myself. I had once believed justice meant my father would go to jail for his crimes. But I was wrong. Just because he was not forced to confront his evil does not mean the little girl inside me did not get justice.

I got justice the second I decided to go for the life I wanted despite what he did to me. I persevered when I realized the longer I stayed quiet, the longer I stayed a victim, and the more control he had over me. My life was his, and the day I stood up and took it back was when I understood true courage. I once heard a young kid say, "Just do it, afraid." Smart kid. Fear is inevitable, but to do it anyway is brave.

As a young girl, it was easy for me to run. I blamed myself for the pain rather than acknowledging the damage. Betrayal by my father gave me an excellent excuse for unacceptable actions. It allowed me to overeat, get drunk daily, do drugs, lash out in rage, withdraw from the world, etc. I pushed people away with my anger, defensiveness, and hatred for myself because I believed they would eventually hate me.

I want something I can never have—a childhood with a dad who loved me, cherished me, laughed with me, cried with me, taught me how to love and respect myself, understood my worth, and helped me see it. This is a debt owed to me that can never be paid.

I understand I can not change my past, but I will always be responsible for changing my future. Growth comes from uncomfortable conversations, trying when you don't think you can, and pretending to love yourself until the day you are no longer pretending.

I can only speak from where I am in life. I am accepting that I am different from others and yet not so different. I have learned to love my quirky qualities. I am grateful my perseverance has helped me cross the finish line of this heart-wrenching tale that some will call a story and I will always know as my life.

Writing this book while processing my pain was tough, but I wouldn't have it any other way. I have worked very hard to get through the deep-rooted pain caused by my father, the man who was supposed to be my hero. I have read countless books, gone to therapy, attended classes, and engaged in journaling, EFT, writing, and much more. My adult life has seemed like a constant attempt to fix the broken child inside.

I think I've done a pretty good job of letting that inner little girl know she is safe and worth it. I no longer cringe when I hear certain sounds or smell familiar scents. I am not brought back to that place when I see a father love his child, nor do I block the stronger emotion I feel when I hear a child's cry.

I am in my mid-thirties as I write this. I have not only survived; I am thriving. I have created an environment filled with trust, love, faith, grace, and hope. I have built my coaching business, Forward Focus LLC, and I am on a mission to help others find their voice in the chaos.

My husband, forever my rock, has proven not all people shy away from a broken soul. My in-laws have shown me love and acceptance in a way I had never known. Family relationships are beginning to mend. I have developed deep friendships. Most importantly, I have proven there is life after internal death.

My heart cries, but this time it's because I finally know true happiness. I will never give up on the little girl inside me who deserves to feel safe and appreciated. She may not have had a father's love, but she has mine, and I made her a promise I will never break.

She will always feel loved and safe and will forever believe she is more than enough. With that, I will share her love with the world so everyone can rise against their nightmares, and together, we can fight for a better life.

If you are a survivor of any kind, you need to accept the power you hold. You choose who you want in your life. Do not feel obligated by family, history, or friends to keep a toxic relationship. I understand this more than ever. I started Forward Focus LLC to help people set boundaries. I now help people become clear on who they are and what they want, then I help them say no to anything that isn't that.

Saying no is not selfish! Whenever you say no to something, you say yes to something else. Another way of putting it is you tolerate what you are not addressing. That is why no matter what I did, my body stayed sick. I was not addressing the source of the heartache; I was tolerating it. I was holding onto his guilt and shame, which wasn't my responsibility.

Boundaries define us—who we are, what we need, and what we can give.

Think of your home. Do you know where your property ends? Of course you do because you don't want to mow your neighbor's yard or shovel their driveway every time it snows. Sure, you're probably willing to help out now and then, but you don't want to do it all the time for every neighbor, and you shouldn't. It is not your responsibility.

And what about your neighbor? Is it okay for them to rummage through your home? Maybe take a peek in your cupboards or underwear drawer, perhaps take your car for a spin?

Of course not! Because there is a clear boundary.

Boundaries are missing in your life if you feel unappreciated, overwhelmed, or timid. We have become so fearful of upsetting people that we don't set the necessary boundaries to help tell the people around us where our property line ends and theirs begins.

It is easy to lose our voice in a world where many speak but do not listen. We quiet our voices to loved ones because not many people can handle a tough discussion, so we hold it in. People will tell us they want the truth, but most want validation.

The good news is none of it matters. You are not responsible for another person's reaction or behavior.

You are responsible for yourself.

Are you a bad person? No? Then why do you believe setting boundaries, saying no, or being honest makes you a bad person? It is time to let that fear go. It's time you show the world what it's been missing—you.

Acknowledgments

To my husband, Lance, a love like yours is what every woman is searching for. Everything I am is because you loved me. Thank you.

To my sister, Keriann, too many years were lost between us, but I am thankful to have found you. You are the most incredible person.

To Sarah, the first person to ever read my story. Thank you! I couldn't have dreamt up a better book coach. You are amazing!

To all my writing buddies from the Mississippi Writers Guild, thank you for your guidance, support, and new friends.

To Chad, I cannot thank you enough for your patience, guidance, trust, encouragement, and support during my healing. Your belief in me allowed me to create a world I never imagined possible.

To my therapist, helping me put down the luggage I had carried for so long freed me up to be who I chose to be. Thanks for giving me a safe space to find my strength.

If you have entered my life at any point, you have impacted my direction. Whether you know it or not, whether our experience was good or not. The bad situations may have been what I needed to become who I am. The good ones may have helped me hold on for one more day. Either way. Thank you.

And finally, I am sorry to those I hurt while I was hurting. You deserved better.

Niki Bergler writes to escape memories of another world to create a world worth enjoying. She resides in Wisconsin with a devilishly handsome husband, and two cats who should have been named Velcro and Opera.

Niki owns Forward Focus LLC. She is a Strategic Intervention Life Coach who focuses on boundaries and healthy relationships. She is also a Specialist in Fitness Nutrition, Motivational Speaker, and now that you are holding this book- an author. How about that?

When she is not lifting people up with her intense, un-caffeinated energy, you can find her volunteering at the food shelter, walking around in search for a bakery, or hanging out in nature doing any number of adrenalizing activities.